Hands-on Graph RAG: Building Advanced Retrieval-Augmented Generation with LLMs

Godfred Llarnas

Preface

In the fast-evolving landscape of artificial intelligence, one of the most exciting developments is the integration of advanced retrieval systems with Large Language Models (LLMs). This combination, known as Retrieval-Augmented Generation (RAG), empowers AI systems to generate contextually rich and highly relevant responses by dynamically retrieving information from external sources. But as datasets grow more complex, and the demand for precision increases, traditional approaches to RAG face significant challenges. This is where graphs step in—offering a structured, scalable, and intuitive way to enhance retrieval systems.

I wrote **"Hands-on Graph RAG: Building Advanced Retrieval-Augmented Generation with LLMs"** to bridge the gap between theory and practice, giving readers the tools they need to understand, build, and optimize Graph RAG pipelines. Whether you're an AI enthusiast, a developer eager to implement cutting-edge technology, or a researcher exploring novel ways to solve complex problems, this book is designed to be your guide.

Why Graphs and RAG?

Throughout my journey in AI development, I've repeatedly seen how critical retrieval systems are for creating intelligent, accurate applications. However, the limitations of flat or unstructured data systems often became glaringly obvious in projects requiring deeper context, richer relationships, or faster performance at scale. Graphs, with their ability to represent relationships as first-class entities, proved transformative.

By combining graphs with LLMs, we can create pipelines that not only retrieve the most relevant data but also understand its context and relationships. This synergy unlocks a world of possibilities—from building smarter recommendation engines to solving domain-specific queries with unparalleled accuracy.

What This Book Offers

This book is intentionally hands-on, blending practical implementation with the underlying theory to ensure you walk away with a deep understanding and the ability to apply what you learn. Here's what you can expect:

- **Clear Explanations**: Complex topics like graph embeddings, semantic search, and RAG architecture are broken down into digestible parts.
- **Step-by-Step Tutorials**: Each chapter guides you through real-world projects, complete with code examples and visual aids.
- **Industry Use Cases**: Discover how Graph RAG is transforming industries like healthcare, finance, and e-commerce.
- **Best Practices**: Learn tips and tricks to optimize performance, debug issues, and scale your solutions effectively.
- **Future Perspectives**: Gain insights into emerging trends and how to prepare for the next wave of AI advancements.

Who This Book Is For

Whether you're new to retrieval-augmented generation or a seasoned AI developer, this book has something for you:

- **Beginners**: Start with foundational concepts and practical examples that build your confidence.
- **Intermediate Developers**: Deepen your knowledge of graph-based retrieval systems and learn to integrate them with LLMs.
- **Experts**: Explore advanced topics and discover how to push the boundaries of what's possible with Graph RAG.

No matter your level, you'll find this book to be a valuable resource for understanding and implementing Graph RAG systems.

A Conversational Approach

I've made a deliberate choice to keep the tone of this book conversational and approachable. AI can be an intimidating field, but it doesn't have to be. I'll share insights, challenges I've faced, and lessons I've learned along the way, so you not only grasp the concepts but also feel inspired to experiment and create.

Think of this book as a dialogue—a collaborative exploration where we unpack the potential of Graph RAG together.

Acknowledgments

This book wouldn't have been possible without the collective wisdom of the AI community and the developers pioneering innovations in graphs and RAG. To the readers diving into this book: thank you for trusting me as your guide on this journey. Your curiosity and drive are what fuel the future of AI.

By the end of this book, my hope is that you'll not only understand the *how* of Graph RAG but also the *why*. You'll leave equipped with the skills to build powerful applications and the vision to imagine new possibilities.

Let's get started!

Table of Contents

Chapter 1: Introduction

1.1 What is Retrieval-Augmented Generation (RAG)?

Large Language Models (LLMs) have revolutionized how we interact with artificial intelligence. These models, trained on massive datasets, are capable of generating human-like text, answering questions, summarizing documents, and much more. However, as impressive as they are, LLMs have inherent limitations. Their knowledge is static—frozen at the time of training—and can sometimes be outdated or incomplete. Worse, they can occasionally "hallucinate," confidently providing false information.

Retrieval-Augmented Generation (RAG) addresses these challenges by creating a dynamic pipeline that combines the power of LLMs with real-time retrieval systems. Let's break this down.

The Basics of RAG

At its core, RAG is a framework that allows an AI system to access external information in real-time to enhance its responses. It does this by integrating two critical components:

1. **Retrieval System**: This is responsible for fetching relevant information from an external knowledge source. These sources can include:
   - Document databases (e.g., PDFs, articles, or wikis)
   - Vector stores containing embeddings of text for similarity searches
   - APIs providing live data (e.g., stock prices, weather updates)
2. **Generation System (LLM)**: Once the retrieval system supplies the relevant context, the LLM uses this information to craft a more accurate, context-aware response.

This synergy ensures that the AI system is no longer constrained by the static knowledge of its training data. Instead, it becomes an adaptable, context-sensitive tool capable of handling queries that demand up-to-date or domain-specific knowledge.

Why is RAG Important?

Let's consider a few scenarios where RAG makes a difference:

1. **Real-Time Knowledge Access**
    Imagine asking an AI for the latest news or today's stock market trends. Without RAG, the LLM would rely solely on its training data, which could be months or years old. With RAG, it retrieves the latest information from a live data source and provides an accurate, timely response.
2. **Domain-Specific Expertise**
    Suppose you're in healthcare, needing precise answers about drug interactions or medical guidelines. Training an LLM exclusively on such specialized data is expensive and resource-intensive. RAG enables the system to query a trusted database, such as PubMed, and generate responses grounded in authoritative sources.
3. **Hallucination Mitigation**
    Traditional LLMs may "invent" facts when they lack the knowledge to answer a query confidently. RAG significantly reduces this risk by anchoring the generation process in retrieved, verified data, making the output more trustworthy.

How RAG Works: A Step-by-Step Process

Here's an overview of how a typical RAG system operates:

1. **Input Query**
    The user submits a query, such as, "What are the symptoms of vitamin D deficiency?"
2. **Retrieval Phase**
    The system processes the query and uses a retrieval mechanism to search its external knowledge sources. These could be structured (e.g., SQL databases) or unstructured (e.g., documents, web pages). The retrieved results, such as relevant medical articles, are ranked and filtered for relevance.
3. **Generation Phase**
    The LLM takes the retrieved content as input and generates a response. For instance, it might combine the retrieved data with its linguistic capabilities to produce a well-structured and human-readable answer.

4. **Final Output**
   The system delivers the enriched response to the user. This process is seamless and often completed in seconds.

RAG in Practice

To better understand RAG's potential, let's look at a few practical applications:

- **Customer Support**: Companies use RAG-powered chatbots to provide customers with accurate, contextual answers by retrieving data from internal knowledge bases.
- **Education**: RAG systems can assist students and researchers by summarizing relevant academic papers or providing explanations from trusted sources.
- **E-Commerce**: Product recommendation engines powered by RAG can use customer preferences and live inventory data to suggest the most suitable items.

Strengths and Limitations of RAG

Strengths

- **Dynamic Knowledge**: Combines the LLM's linguistic capabilities with real-time data retrieval for highly accurate responses.
- **Scalability**: Allows models to function effectively across diverse domains without retraining.
- **Trustworthiness**: Reduces hallucination by grounding responses in retrieved, factual data.

Limitations

- **Dependency on Retrieval Quality**: If the retrieved data is irrelevant or inaccurate, the final response suffers.
- **Latency**: The retrieval step can add slight delays to the generation process, especially for large datasets.

- **Integration Complexity**: Building and optimizing RAG pipelines requires expertise in both retrieval systems and LLMs.

Why Graphs Can Elevate RAG

While traditional retrieval methods are powerful, they often lack the ability to capture the relationships between entities effectively. This is where graphs come in. By representing knowledge as nodes (entities) and edges (relationships), graphs can enhance the retrieval process by prioritizing context and interconnectedness.

For example, in a healthcare application, a graph can link diseases to symptoms, treatments, and risk factors. A RAG system leveraging this graph can retrieve not just a list of symptoms but a holistic, interconnected view of the condition, leading to more insightful responses.

Conclusion

RAG represents a significant leap forward in the field of AI, enabling systems to overcome the static limitations of traditional LLMs. By dynamically integrating retrieval and generation, RAG creates intelligent, context-aware applications with broad utility across industries. As we explore Graph RAG in this book, you'll see how graphs can take this innovation even further, making retrieval smarter, faster, and more insightful.

1.2 Graphs in RAG: An Overview

Retrieval-Augmented Generation (RAG) relies on retrieving the most relevant data to enhance the capabilities of large language models (LLMs). Traditionally, this retrieval has been handled by vector databases or keyword search systems, which perform well for simple queries. However, as the complexity of information and relationships grows, these methods can struggle to provide meaningful context or navigate interconnected data effectively.

This is where **graphs** become a game-changer. By structuring data as interconnected nodes and edges, graphs offer a powerful way to model relationships, context, and hierarchies—features that can significantly enhance the retrieval process in RAG pipelines.

What is a Graph in the Context of RAG?

A graph, in its simplest form, is a data structure consisting of:

- **Nodes (Vertices)**: Represent entities or data points (e.g., people, documents, products).
- **Edges**: Represent the relationships or connections between these nodes (e.g., "knows," "related to," "belongs to").

For instance, imagine a graph of academic research papers. Each paper is a node, and edges represent relationships such as citations, shared authorship, or similar topics. In the context of RAG, such a graph could be used to retrieve not only relevant papers but also related works, contextualizing the results in a meaningful way.

Why Graphs are Essential for RAG

Graphs excel where traditional retrieval systems fall short, particularly in scenarios requiring a deeper understanding of context and relationships. Here's why they're so effective in RAG pipelines:

1. Richer Context Through Relationships

Graphs explicitly represent relationships between data points, allowing for more context-aware retrieval. For example:

- In a customer support application, a graph could link products to their user manuals, FAQs, and troubleshooting guides, enabling the system to retrieve the most relevant resources for a query.
- In a medical knowledge graph, a query about a symptom could surface not just the related disease but also treatments, risk factors, and associated research papers.

This ability to traverse relationships enriches the data retrieved, improving the quality of the final response.

2. Scalability with Interconnected Data

As datasets grow, their complexity increases. Graphs scale well with this complexity, maintaining performance even with millions of nodes and edges. They also enable efficient traversal of interconnected data, ensuring that relevant information is found without exhaustive searches.

3. Enhanced Semantic Understanding

Graphs support embeddings and semantic searches by representing entities in multidimensional space. For instance:

- **Node Embeddings**: Capture the meaning of nodes in relation to their neighbors.
- **Path-Based Retrieval**: Finds information not just directly connected to a query but within a relevant neighborhood or subgraph.

This capability allows graphs to power more intelligent, nuanced queries, especially in knowledge-heavy domains like research, legal, or healthcare.

Graphs in Practice: A Closer Look

Here are a few examples of how graphs transform RAG pipelines:

Example 1: Knowledge Graphs for Domain Expertise

Knowledge graphs are a popular use of graphs in RAG. They organize domain-specific knowledge into interconnected nodes and edges. For instance, a pharmaceutical knowledge graph might include:

- Nodes: Drugs, diseases, symptoms, research papers.
- Edges: Relationships like "treats," "causes," or "cites."

When a query asks, "What drugs can treat migraine headaches?" a graph-based RAG system can retrieve relevant drugs, connected studies, and even alternative treatments through semantic relationships.

Example 2: Personalization in Recommendations

Graphs shine in recommendation systems where personalization is key. For instance:

- In an e-commerce application, a graph could link products to customer reviews, purchase histories, and similar items.
- A RAG system could use this graph to recommend products based on a user's preferences and purchasing behavior, leveraging contextual relationships.

Building Blocks of a Graph RAG System

To integrate graphs into a RAG pipeline, several components come into play:

1. **Graph Database**
   Specialized databases like Neo4j, ArangoDB, or TigerGraph store and manage graph data efficiently. These databases are optimized for querying relationships, making them ideal for RAG.
2. **Graph Embeddings**
   Graph-based machine learning techniques like Graph Neural Networks (GNNs) generate embeddings that represent nodes and relationships in a vector space. These embeddings enable semantic search and similarity-based retrieval.
3. **Query Language**
   Graph query languages like Cypher or Gremlin allow developers to define complex queries that navigate through the graph's structure to find relevant nodes and paths.
4. **Integration with LLMs**
   Once the graph retrieves relevant data, it is passed to the LLM for processing. The LLM uses the retrieved data as context to generate a response, creating a seamless integration between graph-based retrieval and natural language generation.

Advantages of Using Graphs in RAG

Graphs bring several distinct advantages to RAG systems:

- **Dynamic Context**: Graphs adapt to changes in data and relationships, ensuring the retrieval process remains current and relevant.
- **Explainability**: Graphs provide clear insights into how and why specific data points are connected, improving the interpretability of results.
- **Multi-Hop Reasoning**: Graphs support queries that require reasoning across multiple relationships, such as "What are the key studies cited by papers on migraine treatments?"

Challenges and Considerations

Despite their strengths, graphs introduce certain challenges:

- **Complexity**: Building and maintaining graphs can be complex, especially for large datasets.
- **Query Performance**: While graphs are efficient, poorly designed queries or overly dense graphs can impact performance.
- **Integration Overhead**: Combining graphs with traditional RAG components requires expertise in both graph theory and AI pipelines.

However, these challenges can be mitigated with careful design, optimization, and the use of modern graph tools and techniques.

Conclusion

Graphs bring a new dimension to Retrieval-Augmented Generation, enabling systems to move beyond simple keyword-based retrieval to context-aware, relationship-driven intelligence. By structuring data as interconnected nodes and edges, graphs empower RAG pipelines to navigate complex datasets, uncover hidden insights, and deliver more accurate, insightful responses.

1.3 Who This Book is For

Every great book has its audience, and this one is no exception. Whether you're a curious newcomer or a seasoned expert, **"Hands-on Graph RAG: Building Advanced Retrieval-Augmented Generation with LLMs"** is crafted to meet you where you are and help you advance. This chapter outlines the types of readers who will find value in this book and how it caters to their needs.

---

1. Professionals Navigating AI and Data-Driven Industries

If you work in industries like healthcare, finance, e-commerce, or education, you've likely encountered the need for systems that can retrieve accurate, context-aware information quickly. Here's how this book helps you:

- **Healthcare**: Build intelligent systems capable of retrieving clinical guidelines, patient histories, or drug interactions and integrating them seamlessly into LLM-powered chatbots or decision-support tools.
- **Finance**: Use Graph RAG to extract insights from interconnected datasets, such as fraud detection networks or risk assessment models.
- **E-commerce**: Create personalized recommendation engines that leverage the relationships between users, products, and reviews for enhanced customer engagement.
- **Education**: Develop systems that help students or researchers access precise, interconnected information from academic knowledge graphs.

Whether you're a product manager overseeing AI integration or a technical lead implementing the systems, this book equips you with actionable strategies to solve domain-specific challenges.

---

2. AI Enthusiasts and Developers

Are you someone who loves experimenting with cutting-edge technology? Do you enjoy building intelligent applications that push the boundaries of what AI can do? If so, this book is perfect for you.

- **Beginners**: If you're new to Graph RAG, don't worry. This book provides a solid foundation, walking you through essential concepts step-by-step. We start with the basics of graphs, RAG pipelines, and the tools you'll need, ensuring you feel confident as you progress.
- **Intermediate Developers**: For those familiar with RAG or graph-based systems, this book delves deeper into advanced topics like graph embeddings, multi-hop reasoning, and optimization techniques. You'll learn how to design scalable, efficient systems that solve real-world problems.
- **Seasoned Experts**: Even if you're well-versed in AI, this book introduces novel approaches and offers insights into integrating graphs with the latest LLMs. The advanced chapters focus on cutting-edge techniques and emerging trends, ensuring you stay ahead of the curve.

---

3. Researchers Exploring RAG and Graph-Based Systems

If you're a researcher working in AI, natural language processing (NLP), or knowledge representation, you'll find this book to be a practical guide as well as an intellectual resource.

- **Theoretical Exploration**: Gain a deeper understanding of how graphs enhance RAG pipelines, supported by detailed explanations and insightful commentary.
- **Practical Applications**: Learn how to translate theoretical insights into real-world applications, bridging the gap between research and implementation.
- **Emerging Trends**: Stay informed about advancements in graph neural networks (GNNs), knowledge graph construction, and hybrid systems combining graphs and LLMs.

This book provides the tools and examples to help you ground your research in practical, scalable solutions.

---

4. Students and Educators

For students embarking on a journey into AI, NLP, or graph theory, this book offers a comprehensive and accessible introduction to Graph RAG. Similarly, educators can use it as a resource to guide students through hands-on projects or as a supplementary text in advanced AI courses.

- **Hands-On Learning**: Step-by-step tutorials and practical projects help students apply what they learn, reinforcing theoretical concepts through practice.
- **Clear Explanations**: Complex topics like graph embeddings, semantic search, and LLM integration are broken down into digestible sections, making learning engaging and manageable.

Whether you're writing your first Graph RAG application or teaching others how to, this book provides the resources and guidance you need.

5. Industry Innovators and Entrepreneurs

Are you an entrepreneur looking to harness AI to create innovative products? Or perhaps a startup founder exploring ways to differentiate your offering in a competitive market? This book will show you how Graph RAG can give your applications a unique edge.

- **Product Innovation**: Learn how to build intelligent systems that combine LLMs with graph-based retrieval for applications like knowledge assistants, chatbots, and recommendation engines.
- **Business Opportunities**: Discover real-world use cases and industry applications that demonstrate the value of Graph RAG in solving pressing challenges.
- **Rapid Prototyping**: Follow practical guides to quickly prototype and iterate on your ideas, bringing your vision to life faster.

What You Don't Need to Know (Yet)

This book assumes no prior expertise in graph theory, retrieval systems, or RAG pipelines. While some familiarity with AI and programming is helpful, we've designed the content to be approachable for a broad audience. Every technical concept is introduced with clear explanations, and practical examples are included to reinforce learning.

Conclusion

This book is for anyone ready to explore the frontier of AI systems that integrate graphs and LLMs. Whether you're a professional, developer, researcher, student, or entrepreneur, this guide provides the knowledge and tools to help you understand, build, and optimize Graph RAG systems.

1.4 How to Use This Book

This book is more than just a collection of chapters—it's a hands-on guide designed to take you step-by-step through understanding and building Graph RAG systems. Whether you're a beginner eager to learn the basics or an expert looking to refine your skills, this book is structured to meet your needs at every level. Here's how to get the most out of it.

Start at Your Own Level

This book is designed to be flexible, allowing readers of varying experience levels to dive in where they feel most comfortable.

1. **If You're New to RAG or Graph-Based Systems**
   Start at the beginning and work your way through. The early chapters provide the foundational concepts of RAG, an introduction to graphs, and how they enhance retrieval systems. These sections are designed to ease you into the subject with clear explanations and relatable examples.
2. **If You Have Experience with RAG or Graphs**
   Feel free to skip ahead to the more advanced sections, such as building scalable Graph RAG pipelines, integrating graph embeddings, or exploring real-world applications. Each chapter is self-contained, so you won't feel lost if you jump between topics.

3. **If You're Looking for Specific Solutions**
   Use the Table of Contents or Index to locate the topics or techniques you're most interested in. The book is structured to make it easy to find what you need without wading through unrelated content.

How Each Chapter is Structured

Each chapter follows a consistent format to help you learn efficiently:

1. **Introduction**
   A brief overview of the topic, outlining what you'll learn and why it matters.
2. **Concepts and Explanations**
   Detailed but accessible explanations of key ideas, with commentary to provide context and clarity.
3. **Practical Examples**
   Real-world examples and scenarios to illustrate how the concepts are applied in practice.
4. **Key Takeaways**
   A summary of the most important points, helping you consolidate what you've learned.
5. **Actionable Steps**
   Where relevant, you'll find suggestions for how to practice or apply what you've just read, including questions to consider or experiments to try.

Engage with Hands-On Tutorials

This is a **hands-on book**, so be prepared to roll up your sleeves and experiment. Throughout the book, you'll encounter tutorials that guide you through building components of a Graph RAG pipeline. These tutorials are crafted to be incremental:

- **Start Small**: Early examples focus on basic concepts to build your confidence.
- **Grow Gradually**: Later examples integrate multiple concepts, pushing you toward creating more complex systems.

- **Reflect**: After each tutorial, pause to understand how the pieces fit together and how you can extend the functionality further.

Even if you don't plan to code along, reviewing the tutorials will deepen your understanding of how Graph RAG systems work.

Use Case Focus: Real-World Applications

Many chapters include sections on practical applications across industries. These case studies are meant to:

- Show how the techniques you're learning solve real-world problems.
- Inspire ideas for your own projects.
- Provide actionable insights for deploying Graph RAG systems in specific domains like healthcare, e-commerce, or finance.

If you're working on a specific industry problem, these sections will be especially helpful in understanding how to tailor Graph RAG pipelines to meet your needs.

Optimize Your Learning Journey

Here are some tips to make the most of this book:

1. **Take Notes**
   As you work through the chapters, jot down key insights, questions, or ideas for how you might use what you've learned in your own projects.
2. **Experiment Actively**
   Don't just read the tutorials—try them out. Set up a development environment, experiment with the tools, and tweak the examples to see how changes affect the results.
3. **Revisit Concepts**
   Some ideas, like graph embeddings or multi-hop reasoning, can be dense. Don't hesitate to revisit earlier sections if you need a refresher. The book is designed to support iterative learning.

4. **Think Beyond the Book**
   Use the techniques you learn here as building blocks for your own innovations. Graph RAG is a versatile framework, and its applications are limited only by your imagination.

Join the Conversation

This book is part of a larger community effort to explore the potential of Graph RAG. Engage with the community:

- Share your projects and learn from others on forums or GitHub.
- Follow advancements in Graph RAG, graph neural networks, and related technologies.
- Connect with peers who share your interest in building smarter, more context-aware AI systems.

Chapter 2: Foundations of Graphs and RAG

Graph RAG systems combine the power of graph structures with retrieval-augmented generation, enabling smarter, more context-aware applications. Before we dive into building these systems, it's essential to understand the foundational concepts behind graphs, RAG pipelines, and how they work together. This chapter lays the groundwork, providing you with the necessary background to explore and implement Graph RAG effectively.

2.1 Introduction to Graph Theory

Graph theory is the study of graphs—mathematical structures used to model pairwise relationships between objects. At first glance, graphs may seem like abstract constructs, but their applications are deeply embedded in our everyday lives, powering everything from social networks to navigation systems and recommendation engines. In the context of Retrieval-Augmented Generation (RAG), graphs provide a framework for representing data in a way that prioritizes relationships, context, and structure.

Let's explore the fundamental concepts of graph theory and why they are so crucial for enhancing RAG pipelines.

What is a Graph?

A graph is made up of two basic components:

- **Nodes (or Vertices):** These represent the entities in a dataset. For example, in a graph of social connections, each person is a node.
- **Edges:** These represent the relationships between nodes. In the same social graph, edges could represent friendships or professional connections.

Graphs can be visualized as a set of points (nodes) connected by lines (edges), making it easy to see relationships and patterns at a glance.

Types of Graphs

Graphs come in many varieties, each suited to different use cases. Understanding the common types is key to choosing the right structure for your application.

1. Directed vs. Undirected Graphs

- **Directed Graphs (Digraphs):** Edges have a direction, indicating a one-way relationship. For example, in a Twitter graph, an edge from Node A to Node B represents that A follows B, but not necessarily the reverse.
- **Undirected Graphs:** Edges have no direction, representing mutual relationships. In a social graph, a mutual friendship would be represented by an undirected edge.

2. Weighted Graphs

In weighted graphs, edges have weights that represent the strength or importance of the connection. For example:

- In a transportation graph, weights could represent distances or travel times.
- In a recommendation graph, weights might indicate user preference or rating scores.

3. Bipartite Graphs

Bipartite graphs have two distinct sets of nodes, with edges only connecting nodes from different sets. These are common in recommendation systems:

- One set might represent users, and the other set represents products.
- Edges indicate a user's interaction with a product (e.g., a purchase or review).

4. Multigraphs

Multigraphs allow multiple edges between the same pair of nodes, representing different types of relationships. For example, in a knowledge graph about movies, edges might indicate "acted in," "directed," or "produced."

5. Cyclic vs. Acyclic Graphs

- **Cyclic Graphs:** Contain cycles, or paths that loop back to the starting node. These are common in networks like the internet, where hyperlinks form cycles.
- **Acyclic Graphs:** Contain no cycles. Directed Acyclic Graphs (DAGs) are often used in workflows and dependency modeling.

Key Concepts in Graph Theory

Understanding the structure and behavior of graphs requires a few key concepts:

1. Degree

- **Node Degree:** The number of edges connected to a node.
  - In directed graphs, nodes have:
    - **In-Degree:** Number of incoming edges.
    - **Out-Degree:** Number of outgoing edges.
- Example: In a social graph, the in-degree of a node could represent how many people follow them, while the out-degree represents how many they follow.

2. Path

A path is a sequence of nodes connected by edges. Paths can be:

- **Simple Paths:** Contain no repeated nodes or edges.
- **Shortest Paths:** The path between two nodes with the minimum total weight or number of edges.

3. Connected Components

A connected component is a subset of nodes in a graph where every node is reachable from every other node in the subset.

4. Centrality

Centrality measures indicate the importance of a node within a graph. Common types include:

- **Degree Centrality:** Based on the number of connections a node has.
- **Betweenness Centrality:** Based on how often a node appears on the shortest paths between other nodes.
- **Closeness Centrality:** Based on how close a node is to all other nodes in the graph.

Applications of Graph Theory

Graphs are not just theoretical constructs; they have real-world applications across industries:

1. Social Networks

Graphs model relationships between users. They enable features like friend recommendations and influence analysis.

2. Knowledge Graphs

In knowledge representation, graphs connect entities (e.g., people, places, concepts) to create rich, navigable datasets. For example:

- A medical knowledge graph links symptoms to diseases, treatments, and research studies.
- In a search engine, knowledge graphs enhance query understanding by relating terms to their broader context.

3. Recommendation Systems

Graphs link users and products, enabling systems to suggest items based on user preferences and relationships (e.g., "users like you also bought...").

4. Routing and Navigation

Transportation and logistics systems use graphs to calculate optimal routes and schedules.

5. Fraud Detection

In finance, graphs model transactions and relationships between accounts, helping detect suspicious patterns and prevent fraud.

Why Graphs Matter for RAG

Graphs provide capabilities that are uniquely suited to retrieval-augmented generation:

- **Relationship Awareness:** By modeling relationships explicitly, graphs allow RAG systems to retrieve data with richer context.
- **Scalability:** Graphs handle complex, interconnected data efficiently, even at scale.
- **Reasoning and Insights:** Graph algorithms enable multi-hop reasoning and the discovery of hidden connections, enhancing the intelligence of retrieval systems.

For example, in a legal knowledge graph, a query about a court ruling might traverse connections to find related cases, precedents, and laws, creating a comprehensive response.

Conclusion

Graph theory offers a powerful way to represent and analyze relationships in data. By understanding the fundamentals of graph structures and concepts, you gain a versatile toolset for building advanced RAG systems that leverage relationships and context to deliver smarter, more accurate responses.

In the next sections, we'll delve into the basics of RAG pipelines and explore how graphs enhance retrieval, setting the stage for practical implementation.

2.2 Basics of RAG Pipelines

Retrieval-Augmented Generation (RAG) is an innovative approach that combines the strengths of retrieval systems and Large Language Models (LLMs). This combination creates systems capable of producing accurate, contextually enriched, and dynamic responses. To fully appreciate the role of graphs in RAG pipelines, it's essential to first understand how these pipelines function. This section provides a clear and in-depth exploration of the basics of RAG pipelines, breaking down the components, workflows, and benefits.

What is a RAG Pipeline?

A RAG pipeline integrates two key components:

1. **Retrieval System**: Fetches relevant data or context from an external knowledge source.
2. **Generation System (LLM)**: Uses the retrieved data to generate responses tailored to the user's query.

This hybrid approach addresses some inherent limitations of standalone LLMs:

- **Static Knowledge**: LLMs are trained on fixed datasets and lack real-time updates.
- **Hallucination**: LLMs sometimes fabricate information when they lack the context to answer accurately.
- **Domain-Specific Knowledge**: Training LLMs on specialized knowledge is costly and time-intensive.

RAG pipelines resolve these issues by grounding the LLM's output in retrieved, up-to-date, and relevant data.

How a RAG Pipeline Works

A typical RAG pipeline follows these steps:

1. Query Processing

The pipeline starts with a user query. This query may undergo preprocessing to:

- Normalize or tokenize the text.
- Remove unnecessary noise (e.g., stopwords or irrelevant characters).

- Convert the query into a format compatible with the retrieval system, such as embeddings or keywords.

2. Retrieval Phase

The preprocessed query is sent to the retrieval system, which searches for relevant information in an external knowledge base. This knowledge base could be:

- A document database (e.g., articles, manuals, or FAQs).
- A vector store containing semantic embeddings.
- A graph database, where relationships between entities enhance retrieval.

The retrieval system returns a set of ranked results (e.g., the top 5 most relevant documents).

3. Generation Phase

The retrieved data is fed into the LLM as part of the input context. The LLM processes this data along with the original query to:

- Understand the query in the context of the retrieved information.
- Generate a response that combines the retrieved knowledge with the LLM's linguistic capabilities.

4. Output Delivery

The final response, often in natural language, is delivered to the user. Depending on the application, the output might be:

- A detailed answer to a question.
- A summary of retrieved documents.
- A recommendation or decision based on the query.

Key Components of a RAG Pipeline

1. Knowledge Sources

The effectiveness of a RAG pipeline heavily depends on the quality and structure of the knowledge source:

- **Unstructured Text Databases**: Raw text documents stored in traditional or cloud-based systems.
- **Vector Stores**: Semantic embeddings of text data, enabling similarity-based retrieval.
- **Graph Databases**: Data organized as nodes and edges, ideal for capturing relationships and enhancing retrieval.

2. Retrieval Models

Retrieval systems rely on models or algorithms to fetch relevant data. Common approaches include:

- **Keyword-Based Retrieval**: Matches terms in the query with terms in the database. Tools like Elasticsearch and Apache Lucene are popular for this.
- **Embedding-Based Retrieval**: Uses vector representations of text to find semantically similar content. Tools like FAISS (Facebook AI Similarity Search) are often used.
- **Graph-Based Retrieval**: Leverages graph traversal and relationships to locate interconnected, context-rich data.

3. Large Language Models (LLMs)

LLMs like GPT, BERT, or T5 are the backbone of the generation phase. They process the retrieved data and synthesize responses:

- **Pre-Trained Models**: General-purpose models trained on large datasets.
- **Fine-Tuned Models**: Models customized for specific tasks or domains.

Benefits of RAG Pipelines

1. Dynamic and Up-to-Date Responses

Unlike static LLMs, RAG pipelines pull in real-time information from external sources, ensuring responses are current and relevant.

2. Reduced Hallucination

By grounding the generation process in retrieved data, RAG pipelines significantly lower the chances of LLMs inventing false information.

3. Enhanced Domain Expertise

Instead of retraining an LLM for every domain, RAG pipelines retrieve specialized knowledge from domain-specific sources, making them cost-effective and flexible.

4. Scalability

RAG systems can scale across multiple domains by connecting to different retrieval systems or knowledge bases, making them versatile for various applications.

Challenges in RAG Pipelines

While powerful, RAG pipelines are not without their challenges:

- **Retrieval Quality**: The system's effectiveness hinges on retrieving relevant, accurate data. Irrelevant results can degrade the quality of the final response.
- **Integration Complexity**: Combining retrieval systems and LLMs requires careful engineering to ensure compatibility and performance.
- **Latency**: The retrieval phase can introduce delays, particularly with large or complex knowledge sources.
- **Data Maintenance**: Keeping knowledge bases up to date and accurate requires ongoing effort.

Real-World Applications of RAG Pipelines

1. Customer Support

RAG systems enhance chatbots and virtual assistants by retrieving product manuals, FAQs, and troubleshooting guides to answer user queries.

2. Research Assistance

Researchers use RAG systems to summarize relevant papers, pull citations, or find related work in their field.

3. Healthcare

Medical applications leverage RAG to retrieve clinical guidelines, patient histories, and research studies for better decision-making support.

4. E-Commerce

RAG pipelines power personalized recommendation systems by retrieving relevant product details, reviews, and inventory updates.

2.3 The Role of Graphs in Enhancing Retrieval

Graphs fundamentally change the way retrieval systems function, offering a structured and relationship-focused approach to finding and organizing information. In Retrieval-Augmented Generation (RAG) systems, the inclusion of graphs transforms retrieval into a more context-aware and insightful process, ensuring that data not only matches the query but also reflects meaningful connections and relevance.

Moving Beyond Traditional Retrieval

Traditional retrieval systems, such as keyword-based searches or vector similarity methods, perform well for straightforward queries. However, they often fall short in handling complex, interconnected datasets or queries requiring nuanced understanding. For example, if you ask, "What is the relationship between diabetes and hypertension?" a keyword-based system might return documents mentioning both terms but fail to capture the intricate medical correlations between the two.

Graphs address these challenges by representing data as nodes (entities) and edges (relationships). This structure allows for richer, more meaningful retrieval by leveraging the connections between pieces of information.

How Graphs Enhance Retrieval

Graphs bring several unique capabilities to RAG pipelines:

1. Relationship-Centric Retrieval
Graphs explicitly model relationships, which means they don't just store entities but also how they interact. This makes them ideal for questions that depend on understanding these interactions. For instance:

- In a legal domain, a graph can link court cases to precedents, related statutes, and legal scholars' opinions, enabling retrieval that surfaces relevant cases alongside their context.
- In a healthcare setting, a graph can link symptoms, diseases, treatments, and research papers, providing a network of interconnected knowledge.

2. Contextual Exploration
Graphs enable traversal through relationships, allowing the retrieval system to explore data in a way that mimics human reasoning. For example, a query about a particular author in an academic graph could traverse connections to their published works, citations, and collaborators, creating a holistic view of their contributions.

3. Semantic Understanding through Graph Embeddings
Graphs can represent nodes and relationships in a vectorized form through embeddings. These embeddings allow for similarity-based searches that go beyond exact matches, enabling the system to find semantically related content. For instance, a graph-based system might recognize that "heart disease" and "cardiovascular conditions" are related concepts and retrieve relevant data even if the terms don't explicitly match the query.

4. Multi-Hop Reasoning
Multi-hop reasoning allows the system to connect the dots across multiple relationships. In a knowledge graph, a query about "renewable energy investments in Europe" might involve traversing from renewable energy technologies to companies, from companies to investment portfolios, and finally filtering for European entities. This layered reasoning creates depth and relevance in retrieval.

5. Scalability and Adaptability

Graphs excel at handling large, interconnected datasets without significant performance degradation. They can also adapt as relationships evolve, making them particularly valuable for dynamic domains such as finance or social networks.

Applications of Graphs in RAG Systems

Graphs are especially impactful in domains where relationships and context are central to understanding and decision-making:

In **customer support**, graphs can link products to user manuals, troubleshooting steps, and FAQs. When a customer asks about a specific error, the system can retrieve the most relevant information, including related issues and solutions.

In **healthcare**, a graph-based system can retrieve interconnected insights about a disease, linking symptoms, treatments, and ongoing research. For instance, querying about a treatment might surface clinical trial results, known side effects, and compatible therapies.

In **e-commerce**, a graph can model relationships between products, users, and reviews. A query about a specific product might retrieve not just its details but also complementary products, related customer reviews, and frequently purchased bundles.

Challenges of Integrating Graphs

While graphs are powerful, integrating them into RAG systems comes with challenges. Building and maintaining a graph requires thoughtful design to ensure the relationships it represents are accurate and meaningful. Poorly constructed graphs can lead to irrelevant or misleading results, undermining the system's effectiveness. Additionally, the computational demands of querying large graphs and performing complex traversals must be carefully managed to avoid latency issues.

Conclusion

Graphs elevate retrieval in RAG systems by making it relationship-driven, context-aware, and semantically rich. By representing data as interconnected nodes and edges, graphs enable retrieval systems to uncover deeper insights and deliver more accurate and meaningful results. As we move into practical implementation, understanding how to design and utilize graphs effectively is key to unlocking their full potential in RAG pipelines.

2.4 Graph Databases and Tools Overview

Graphs are powerful tools for modeling relationships and context, but their true potential is unlocked through graph databases. These databases are specifically designed to store, manage, and query graph-structured data efficiently. They provide the foundation for integrating graphs into Retrieval-Augmented Generation (RAG) pipelines, enabling enhanced retrieval and reasoning capabilities.

This section explores the fundamentals of graph databases, highlights some of the most popular tools, and provides insights into how to choose the right one for your needs.

What Are Graph Databases?

Graph databases are specialized databases optimized to handle graph data structures. Unlike relational databases, which use tables and rows, graph databases store data as nodes (entities) and edges (relationships). This structure allows for quick and efficient queries, especially when relationships between data points are central to the task.

For example, in a graph database of academic papers, nodes might represent papers, authors, and topics, while edges capture relationships like "authored by," "cites," or "relates to." Queries can then traverse these edges to find related papers or authors in a way that traditional databases cannot match.

Why Use Graph Databases in RAG Pipelines?

Graph databases are ideal for RAG systems because they excel at handling complex, interconnected data. Their ability to navigate relationships and uncover context makes them perfect for tasks like multi-hop reasoning, semantic search, and retrieving contextually rich data.

In a RAG pipeline, a graph database acts as the retrieval system. It quickly finds and returns relevant nodes and their relationships, providing the LLM with richer context for generating responses. This integration is particularly valuable for applications like knowledge graphs, recommendation systems, and real-time decision-making tools.

Popular Graph Databases

The landscape of graph databases is diverse, with each tool offering unique features and strengths. Below are some of the most popular options:

Neo4j
Neo4j is one of the most widely used graph databases, known for its user-friendly interface and robust querying capabilities. It uses Cypher, a SQL-like query language, to make graph traversal intuitive. Neo4j is ideal for building knowledge graphs, recommendation systems, and fraud detection pipelines.

TigerGraph
TigerGraph specializes in handling large-scale graph data and performing complex analytics. Its performance and scalability make it a strong choice for applications like real-time fraud detection, supply chain optimization, and personalized healthcare.

Dgraph
Dgraph is a distributed, horizontally scalable graph database. It uses GraphQL as its query language, making it accessible to developers familiar with web technologies. Dgraph is excellent for projects requiring fast, scalable graph queries.

ArangoDB
ArangoDB is a multi-model database that supports graphs, documents, and

key-value pairs. Its versatility makes it a good option for projects that require combining graph data with other types of data models.

Amazon Neptune
Amazon Neptune is a fully managed graph database service integrated with AWS. It supports multiple graph query languages, including Gremlin and SPARQL, and is well-suited for applications already hosted in AWS environments.

Choosing the Right Graph Database

Selecting the best graph database depends on several factors:

- **Scalability Needs:** For small-scale projects, Neo4j's simplicity may be sufficient. For larger datasets and real-time analytics, TigerGraph or Dgraph might be better suited.
- **Ease of Use:** Neo4j's Cypher query language is intuitive, while Dgraph's use of GraphQL appeals to developers familiar with modern web development.
- **Integration Requirements:** Amazon Neptune integrates seamlessly with other AWS services, making it a logical choice for cloud-native applications.
- **Query Complexity:** Applications requiring advanced graph traversals and analytics may benefit from TigerGraph's performance optimizations.

Graph Query Languages

Graph databases are accessed and queried through specialized languages designed for navigating nodes and edges. Some of the most common include:

- **Cypher (Neo4j):** Cypher is designed for simplicity and readability, making it easy to express complex queries.
- **Gremlin (Apache TinkerPop):** Gremlin is versatile and supports graph traversals in a functional programming style.

- **GraphQL (Dgraph, others):** GraphQL is widely used for building APIs and integrates graph data seamlessly into web applications.
- **SPARQL:** SPARQL is used for querying RDF (Resource Description Framework) graphs, often in semantic web and linked data contexts.

Each language has its strengths, and the choice depends on the database and the specific requirements of your application.

Integration with RAG Pipelines

Integrating a graph database into a RAG pipeline involves several steps. First, the graph database is populated with data relevant to the application, whether from structured datasets, unstructured text, or other sources. Next, queries are designed to extract relevant nodes and edges based on the user's query. Finally, the retrieved data is passed to the LLM for context-aware generation.

For example, in a customer support application, a graph database might store relationships between products, FAQs, and troubleshooting steps. When a user asks about a specific product issue, the system queries the graph to retrieve the most relevant resources, which the LLM uses to craft a detailed response.

Conclusion

Graph databases are essential tools for building advanced RAG systems, offering unparalleled capabilities for managing and querying relational data. By choosing the right database and query language for your needs, you can unlock the full potential of graphs in enhancing retrieval and creating smarter, more context-aware applications. With these tools in hand, you're ready to take the next step in designing and implementing powerful Graph RAG pipelines.

Chapter 3: Building Graph-Enhanced RAG Pipelines

Now that you understand the foundations of graphs and their role in enhancing retrieval, it's time to build a functional Graph RAG pipeline. This chapter walks you through the key components of a Graph RAG system, the design of knowledge graphs, their integration with LLMs, and concludes with a case study that ties everything together. By the end of this chapter, you'll have a clear blueprint for creating your own pipeline.

3.1 Key Components of a Graph RAG System

A Graph RAG system brings together the complementary strengths of graphs and LLMs to create a robust framework for context-rich retrieval and intelligent response generation. To fully appreciate how these systems work, let's explore the key components that form their backbone.

Graph Database: The Structural Foundation

At the heart of a Graph RAG system is the graph database, a specialized data store designed to handle graph-structured data. Unlike traditional relational databases, a graph database focuses on relationships, storing data as nodes (entities) and edges (connections). This structure enables fast and efficient querying, especially for tasks involving complex relationships or multi-hop reasoning.

When I first started working with graph databases, I was struck by how intuitive they felt compared to traditional databases. For instance, instead of sifting through multiple tables to understand how two entities were connected, I could query a graph database and immediately see the relationships in a visually compelling way. This clarity is one of the reasons graphs are so powerful in RAG pipelines.

Knowledge Graph: The Heart of the System

The knowledge graph is more than just a dataset; it's a thoughtfully designed map of information that models a specific domain. It organizes entities and their relationships into a structured format, making it easier for the system to retrieve relevant data.

Imagine a healthcare application. A knowledge graph in this domain might have nodes representing diseases, symptoms, treatments, and medical articles, with edges capturing relationships like "causes," "treated by," or "cited by." This interconnected web of information enables the system to retrieve not just isolated data points but context-rich insights.

One lesson I've learned from designing knowledge graphs is the importance of focusing on the relationships that matter most to your use case. Including every possible connection might seem tempting, but it often leads to unnecessary complexity. Instead, prioritizing the relationships that directly support your retrieval goals ensures the graph remains manageable and effective.

Query Engine: The Bridge to the Graph

The query engine is the tool that translates user queries into graph queries and retrieves the most relevant information. It serves as the interface between the user's intent and the graph database.

Graph query languages like Cypher (used by Neo4j) and Gremlin (Apache TinkerPop) make it easy to express complex searches. For instance, querying a graph for "all treatments for Type 2 diabetes with high effectiveness" becomes a straightforward command. When I first explored these query languages, I was amazed at how naturally they aligned with the way I thought about relationships and paths in data.

A well-designed query engine not only fetches relevant data but also ensures it is ranked and filtered for quality. This step is critical, as the data retrieved here will form the foundation of the system's final response.

Preprocessing Pipeline: Making Data Usable

Data retrieved from the graph is often raw and needs preprocessing before being passed to the LLM. This pipeline transforms structured graph data into context-rich text or embeddings that the LLM can understand.

For example, if the graph query retrieves:

- Node: "Type 2 diabetes"
- Edge: "treated by"
- Target Node: "Metformin"

The preprocessing pipeline might convert this into:
"Type 2 diabetes is treated with Metformin. It is a highly effective first-line treatment recommended by clinical guidelines."

When building preprocessing pipelines, I've found that clarity and simplicity are key. Overloading the LLM with too much information can dilute its ability to generate meaningful responses. Instead, focus on crafting concise, relevant inputs that highlight the most important connections.

Large Language Model (LLM): The Generative Powerhouse

The LLM is the system's brain, responsible for transforming retrieved data into coherent, context-aware responses. It combines its pre-trained knowledge with the input from the graph to deliver high-quality outputs.

One of the most impressive things about LLMs is their ability to contextualize and articulate complex information. When paired with graph data, they excel at synthesizing structured relationships into natural language, providing users with answers that feel human and intuitive.

However, the LLM is only as good as the input it receives. Feeding it well-structured and relevant data from the graph ensures that it generates responses that are both accurate and meaningful.

Integration Layer: The Glue That Binds

The integration layer orchestrates the entire pipeline, ensuring seamless communication between components. It manages the flow of data, from user queries to graph retrieval and LLM generation, and ensures the system operates efficiently.

In my experience, the integration layer often involves a mix of APIs, middleware, and orchestration tools. While it might not be the most glamorous part of the system, it's the unsung hero that keeps everything running smoothly. A robust integration layer can handle tasks like error handling, caching, and query optimization, ensuring the system remains responsive and reliable.

Conclusion

Building a Graph RAG system is like assembling a symphony of interconnected parts. Each component—the graph database, knowledge graph, query engine, preprocessing pipeline, LLM, and integration layer—plays a critical role in ensuring the system functions as intended.

By understanding these components and how they work together, you're well on your way to designing and building your own Graph RAG pipelines. In the next sections, we'll dive deeper into the practical aspects of creating knowledge graphs and integrating them with LLMs, bringing theory into practice.

3.2 Designing and Connecting Knowledge Graphs

Designing a knowledge graph is the art of structuring complex, interconnected information in a way that aligns with a specific purpose. A well-designed knowledge graph enhances retrieval, promotes clarity, and enables intelligent systems like Graph RAG to deliver meaningful insights. This section will guide you through the process of designing and connecting knowledge graphs, blending theory, practical steps, and a complete working code example.

Why Knowledge Graphs Matter

Knowledge graphs are more than just data structures; they're tools for understanding and reasoning. Unlike flat datasets or tables, a knowledge graph captures relationships and context, enabling multi-hop reasoning and complex queries. This capability makes them essential for domains like healthcare, legal, finance, and more.

From my experience, designing a good knowledge graph starts with asking the right questions:

- What domain are you modeling?
- Who will use this graph, and for what purpose?
- What relationships are critical to surface meaningful insights?

Answering these questions helps focus your efforts and keeps the graph manageable and purposeful.

Steps to Design a Knowledge Graph

1. Define the Scope

Start by outlining the domain and goals of your graph. A healthcare graph, for instance, might include entities like diseases, symptoms, treatments, and research papers.

2. Identify Entities and Relationships

List the key entities (nodes) and relationships (edges) in your domain. For example:

- Entities: "Type 2 diabetes," "Metformin," "Glucose levels."
- Relationships: "treated by," "caused by," "associated with."

3. Choose a Graph Database

Select a graph database that aligns with your technical requirements. For this example, we'll use **Neo4j**, a popular and user-friendly option.

4. Load and Structure Data

Prepare your data by cleaning and organizing it into a format suitable for graph ingestion. CSV files are often a good starting point.

5. Test Queries

Run sample queries to ensure the graph retrieves meaningful results. Queries should reflect real-world questions users might ask.

6. Optimize

Refine the graph's structure, relationships, and indexing based on performance and feedback.

Practical Implementation: Building a Knowledge Graph with Neo4j

Step 1: Install and Set Up Neo4j

1. Download and install Neo4j from the official website.
2. Start the Neo4j Desktop application and create a new database.
3. Note the credentials for accessing the database (username and password).

Step 2: Prepare Your Data

Let's use a simplified healthcare dataset with diseases, symptoms, and treatments:

diseases.csv

id	name
D1	Type 2 Diabetes
D2	Hypertension

symptoms.csv

id	name
S1	High Glucose
S2	High BP

treatments.csv

id	name
T1	Metformin
T2	Beta Blockers

relationships.csv

from_id	to_id	relationship
D1	S1	has_symptom
D2	S2	has_symptom
D1	T1	treated_by
D2	T2	treated_by

Step 3: Write the Code

Here's a Python script to create and populate the graph using Neo4j's Python driver:

```python
---
from neo4j import GraphDatabase

# Neo4j connection details
uri = "bolt://localhost:7687"
username = "neo4j"
password = "password"

# Initialize the Neo4j driver
driver = GraphDatabase.driver(uri, auth=(username, password))

# Function to create nodes
def create_nodes(tx, label, nodes):
    for node in nodes:
        query = f"CREATE (n:{label} {{id: $id, name:
$name}})"
```

```
        tx.run(query, id=node["id"], name=node["name"])

# Function to create relationships
def create_relationships(tx, relationships):
    for rel in relationships:
        query = """
        MATCH (a {id: $from_id}), (b {id: $to_id})
        CREATE (a)-[:{relationship}]->(b)
        """
        tx.run(query, from_id=rel["from_id"],
to_id=rel["to_id"], relationship=rel["relationship"])

# Data preparation
diseases = [{"id": "D1", "name": "Type 2 Diabetes"}, {"id":
"D2", "name": "Hypertension"}]
symptoms = [{"id": "S1", "name": "High Glucose"}, {"id":
"S2", "name": "High BP"}]
treatments = [{"id": "T1", "name": "Metformin"}, {"id": "T2",
"name": "Beta Blockers"}]
relationships = [
    {"from_id": "D1", "to_id": "S1", "relationship":
"HAS_SYMPTOM"},
    {"from_id": "D2", "to_id": "S2", "relationship":
"HAS_SYMPTOM"},
    {"from_id": "D1", "to_id": "T1", "relationship":
"TREATED_BY"},
    {"from_id": "D2", "to_id": "T2", "relationship":
"TREATED_BY"}
]

# Populate the graph
with driver.session() as session:
    session.write_transaction(create_nodes, "Disease",
diseases)
    session.write_transaction(create_nodes, "Symptom",
symptoms)
    session.write_transaction(create_nodes, "Treatment",
treatments)
    session.write_transaction(create_relationships,
relationships)

print("Graph successfully populated!")
driver.close()
```

Step 4: Test Queries

Use Cypher to query the graph. For example:

```
cypher
```

```
---
MATCH (d:Disease)-[:HAS_SYMPTOM]->(s:Symptom)
RETURN d.name AS Disease, s.name AS Symptom
```

This will return:

Disease	Symptom
Type 2 Diabetes	High Glucose
Hypertension	High BP

Tips for Success

1. **Start Simple**: Build a small graph and expand as you validate the structure and relationships.
2. **Focus on Queries**: Think about the questions your graph should answer. This will guide your design choices.
3. **Iterate**: A knowledge graph evolves over time. Continuously refine it based on user feedback and new data.

Conclusion

Designing and connecting knowledge graphs is both an art and a science. By focusing on the structure, relationships, and practical applications, you can create a graph that adds significant value to your RAG pipeline. With tools like Neo4j and Python, the process becomes not only manageable but also enjoyable. In the next section, we'll explore how to integrate these graphs with LLMs to unlock their full potential.

3.3 Integrating Graphs with LLMs

Integrating graphs with Large Language Models (LLMs) combines the relationship-focused power of graphs with the generative capabilities of LLMs. This synergy enables the creation of intelligent systems that retrieve context-rich data from graphs and use it to generate accurate, meaningful, and human-like responses.

This guide provides a deep dive into the integration process, highlighting key concepts, practical use cases, and step-by-step implementation with well-documented code.

Why Integrate Graphs with LLMs?

Graphs excel at representing and retrieving structured relationships, while LLMs are adept at understanding and generating natural language. Integrating the two creates systems that:

- Retrieve highly relevant, context-aware data by leveraging graph structures.
- Generate coherent, detailed responses by grounding LLM outputs in graph data.
- Enable advanced use cases like multi-hop reasoning, semantic search, and domain-specific query handling.

For example, in a healthcare application, a graph database might retrieve relationships between diseases, symptoms, and treatments. An LLM can then use this retrieved data to generate a response to a patient's query, such as "What treatments are available for Type 2 diabetes?"

Steps to Integrate Graphs with LLMs

1. Formulate the Query

The integration starts with a user's input query. This query must be preprocessed to extract intent and key entities that guide the graph retrieval process.

2. Query the Graph

The preprocessed query is translated into a graph query using a graph query language like Cypher or Gremlin. The query retrieves nodes and edges relevant to the user's intent.

3. Preprocess Retrieved Data

The graph query's output, often in a structured format, needs to be converted into text or embeddings that the LLM can understand. This step includes:

- Concatenating retrieved relationships into coherent sentences.
- Summarizing or filtering the retrieved data.

4. Use the LLM for Generation

The preprocessed graph data is passed to the LLM as part of its input context. The LLM combines this data with its generative capabilities to produce a response.

5. Deliver the Response

The final response is formatted and delivered to the user. This step may involve reformatting the output to match the desired tone or structure.

Practical Implementation

Here's a practical example that integrates a Neo4j graph database with an LLM (e.g., OpenAI's GPT-3). The example uses Python for implementation.

Step 1: Install Dependencies

Install the required libraries:

```bash
---
pip install neo4j openai
```

Step 2: Set Up Neo4j

Ensure your Neo4j database is running and populated with data. For this example, we'll use a healthcare knowledge graph with diseases, symptoms, and treatments.

Step 3: Define the Integration Code

The following Python script demonstrates the integration:

```python
---
from neo4j import GraphDatabase
import openai

# Neo4j connection details
NEO4J_URI = "bolt://localhost:7687"
NEO4J_USER = "neo4j"
NEO4J_PASSWORD = "password"

# OpenAI API key
OPENAI_API_KEY = "your_openai_api_key"
openai.api_key = OPENAI_API_KEY

# Initialize Neo4j driver
driver = GraphDatabase.driver(NEO4J_URI, auth=(NEO4J_USER,
NEO4J_PASSWORD))

# Function to query the graph database
def query_graph(query):
    with driver.session() as session:
        result = session.run(query)
        return [record for record in result]

# Function to preprocess graph data for LLM
def preprocess_data(graph_data):
    sentences = []
    for record in graph_data:
        disease = record.get("disease")
        treatment = record.get("treatment")
        symptom = record.get("symptom")
        sentences.append(
            f"The disease {disease} is treated by {treatment}
and is associated with the symptom {symptom}."
        )
    return " ".join(sentences)

# Function to generate response using LLM
def generate_response(prompt):
    response = openai.Completion.create(
        engine="text-davinci-003",
        prompt=prompt,
        max_tokens=150,
    )
    return response.choices[0].text.strip()
```

```
# User query
user_query = "What treatments are available for Type 2
diabetes?"

# Step 1: Formulate and execute graph query
graph_query = """
MATCH (d:Disease {name: 'Type 2 Diabetes'})-[:HAS_SYMPTOM]-
>(s:Symptom),
      (d)-[:TREATED_BY]->(t:Treatment)
RETURN d.name AS disease, t.name AS treatment, s.name AS
symptom
"""
graph_data = query_graph(graph_query)

# Step 2: Preprocess graph data
context = preprocess_data(graph_data)

# Step 3: Combine user query and graph data for LLM
prompt = f"User query: {user_query}\nContext:
{context}\nAnswer:"
response = generate_response(prompt)

# Step 4: Output the response
print("Response:", response)

# Close the Neo4j connection
driver.close()
```

Step 4: Run the Code

When you run the code, the pipeline will:

1. Query the graph database for relevant nodes and relationships.
2. Preprocess the retrieved data into a context-rich prompt.
3. Use the LLM to generate a coherent response.
4. Deliver the response to the user.

Expected Output

For the user query, "What treatments are available for Type 2 diabetes?", the system might generate a response like:

"Type 2 diabetes is commonly treated with Metformin, which is highly effective. It is also associated with the symptom of high glucose levels."

Best Practices for Integration

- **Design Queries Thoughtfully:** Ensure graph queries retrieve relevant and concise data.
- **Limit Input Length:** LLMs have token limits. Preprocess graph data to include only the most critical information.
- **Test Iteratively:** Run various queries to refine the integration and ensure quality results.
- **Handle Errors Gracefully:** Include error handling for cases where the graph query returns no results or the LLM fails to generate a response.

Conclusion

Integrating graphs with LLMs unlocks the full potential of both technologies, enabling systems that are both intelligent and intuitive. By following a structured approach and leveraging tools like Neo4j and OpenAI, you can build Graph RAG pipelines that deliver meaningful, context-rich responses. In the next section, we'll apply these concepts in a comprehensive case study to solidify your understanding.

3.4 Case Study: A Simple Graph RAG Pipeline

To truly understand the power of a Graph RAG (Retrieval-Augmented Generation) pipeline, let's dive into a practical example. This case study will walk you through building a basic Graph RAG pipeline step-by-step, integrating a Neo4j knowledge graph with an OpenAI LLM to answer user queries in the healthcare domain. The goal is to create a system that retrieves relevant information from a graph database and generates a natural language response using an LLM.

Case Overview

We'll build a pipeline that answers user queries about diseases, their symptoms, and available treatments. For instance, when a user asks, "What are the treatments for Type 2 diabetes?", the system will retrieve relevant data from a knowledge graph and generate a coherent, context-rich response.

Step 1: Set Up the Environment

First, ensure you have the required tools and libraries installed.

Install Dependencies

```bash
---
pip install neo4j openai
```

Start the Neo4j Database

1. Download and install Neo4j from the official website.
2. Create and start a new database.
3. Load the sample data provided below.

Step 2: Build the Knowledge Graph

Create the Sample Data

Use the following Cypher queries to populate the Neo4j database:

```cypher
---
// Create Disease Nodes
CREATE (d1:Disease {name: "Type 2 Diabetes"})
CREATE (d2:Disease {name: "Hypertension"})

// Create Symptom Nodes
CREATE (s1:Symptom {name: "High Glucose"})
CREATE (s2:Symptom {name: "High Blood Pressure"})

// Create Treatment Nodes
```

```
CREATE (t1:Treatment {name: "Metformin"})
CREATE (t2:Treatment {name: "Beta Blockers"})

// Create Relationships
MATCH (d1:Disease {name: "Type 2 Diabetes"}), (s1:Symptom
{name: "High Glucose"})
CREATE (d1)-[:HAS_SYMPTOM]->(s1)

MATCH (d1:Disease {name: "Type 2 Diabetes"}), (t1:Treatment
{name: "Metformin"})
CREATE (d1)-[:TREATED_BY]->(t1)

MATCH (d2:Disease {name: "Hypertension"}), (s2:Symptom {name:
"High Blood Pressure"})
CREATE (d2)-[:HAS_SYMPTOM]->(s2)

MATCH (d2:Disease {name: "Hypertension"}), (t2:Treatment
{name: "Beta Blockers"})
CREATE (d2)-[:TREATED_BY]->(t2)
```

Step 3: Connect to Neo4j

Initialize the Neo4j Driver

```python
---
from neo4j import GraphDatabase

# Connection details
NEO4J_URI = "bolt://localhost:7687"
NEO4J_USER = "neo4j"
NEO4J_PASSWORD = "your_password"

# Initialize the driver
driver = GraphDatabase.driver(NEO4J_URI, auth=(NEO4J_USER,
NEO4J_PASSWORD))
```

Step 4: Query the Knowledge Graph

Write a Function to Fetch Data

```python
---
def query_graph(disease_name):
    query = """
```

```
    MATCH (d:Disease {name: $disease_name})-[:HAS_SYMPTOM]-
>(s:Symptom),
          (d)-[:TREATED_BY]->(t:Treatment)
    RETURN d.name AS disease, s.name AS symptom, t.name AS
treatment
    """
    with driver.session() as session:
        results = session.run(query,
disease_name=disease_name)
        return [record for record in results]

# Example usage
data = query_graph("Type 2 Diabetes")
print(data)
```

This query retrieves symptoms and treatments related to a specific disease.

Step 5: Preprocess the Retrieved Data

Transform Data for LLM Input

```python
---
def preprocess_data(graph_data):
    sentences = []
    for record in graph_data:
        disease = record["disease"]
        symptom = record["symptom"]
        treatment = record["treatment"]
        sentences.append(
            f"{disease} is associated with the symptom
{symptom} and is treated with {treatment}."
        )
    return " ".join(sentences)

# Preprocess the graph data
context = preprocess_data(data)
print(context)
```

Step 6: Integrate with OpenAI's LLM

Set Up the OpenAI API

```python
```

```
---
import openai

# Set your OpenAI API key
openai.api_key = "your_openai_api_key"
Generate a Response
python
---
def generate_response(user_query, context):
    prompt = f"User query: {user_query}\nContext:
{context}\nAnswer:"
    response = openai.Completion.create(
        engine="text-davinci-003",
        prompt=prompt,
        max_tokens=150
    )
    return response.choices[0].text.strip()

# Generate a response
user_query = "What are the treatments for Type 2 diabetes?"
response = generate_response(user_query, context)
print("Response:", response)
```

Step 7: Deliver the Final Output

When the user asks, "What are the treatments for Type 2 diabetes?", the pipeline produces a response like:

"Type 2 diabetes is associated with the symptom High Glucose and is treated with Metformin. Metformin is a highly effective treatment commonly recommended by healthcare professionals."

Best Practices

- **Optimize Queries:** Refine graph queries to fetch only the most relevant data.
- **Limit Context Length:** Ensure the preprocessed data doesn't exceed the token limits of the LLM.
- **Test Thoroughly:** Run the pipeline with diverse queries to validate accuracy and robustness.

Conclusion

This case study demonstrates how to create a simple yet powerful Graph RAG pipeline by integrating Neo4j with OpenAI's LLM. By following these steps, you can adapt the pipeline to various domains and build intelligent, context-aware systems. As you scale, consider adding advanced features like multi-hop reasoning and real-time updates to enhance functionality further.

Chapter 4: Tools and Technologies

Building a Graph RAG pipeline requires a solid foundation of tools and technologies. This chapter explores the key resources you'll need, from setting up a development environment to selecting the right databases and libraries. By the end of this chapter, you'll have a clear understanding of the tools available and how to choose the best fit for your specific needs.

4.1 Setting Up Your Development Environment

Setting up your development environment is a crucial first step in building a Graph RAG pipeline. A properly configured environment ensures smooth experimentation, debugging, and deployment of your project. This guide walks you through creating an efficient and scalable setup for working with graph databases and LLMs.

Key Components of a Development Environment

At the core of your environment are the tools and frameworks needed to manage graphs, integrate with LLMs, and process data effectively.

- **Graph Database**: Install and configure a graph database like Neo4j or Dgraph to store and query relationships in your data.
- **Programming Language**: Python is the preferred choice due to its rich ecosystem of libraries for graph processing, data manipulation, and LLM integration.
- **LLM Integration**: Set up access to an LLM platform like OpenAI or Hugging Face Transformers.
- **Development Tools**: Use an IDE, version control, and containerization tools to streamline coding and deployment.

Step-by-Step Setup

Install Python and Essential Libraries

Ensure you have Python 3.8 or later installed. Install essential libraries for graph databases, LLMs, and data processing:

```bash
pip install neo4j openai pandas numpy
```

These libraries provide the core functionality to interact with Neo4j, process graph data, and connect with OpenAI's API.

Set Up Neo4j

1. **Download and Install Neo4j**
   Visit the Neo4j website and download the Community Edition or Desktop version. Follow the installation instructions for your operating system.
2. **Start the Database**
   Launch the Neo4j database and set up a new project. Note the connection details, including the Bolt URL (e.g., `bolt://localhost:7687`), username, and password.
3. **Test the Connection**
   Use the Neo4j Browser interface to run a simple query:

```cypher
RETURN "Hello, Neo4j!"
```

If you see a successful result, your database is ready to use.

Set Up an IDE

Choose an Integrated Development Environment (IDE) that fits your workflow. **VS Code** is highly recommended for Python development due to its rich ecosystem of extensions.

- **Install Python Extension**: Add the Python extension in VS Code for syntax highlighting, linting, and debugging support.
- **Install Neo4j Extension**: If you use Neo4j, the Neo4j extension for VS Code provides easy access to query visualization.

Configure the OpenAI API

1. **Create an OpenAI Account**
   Sign up at <u>OpenAI</u> and obtain your API key from the dashboard.
2. **Install OpenAI Python SDK**
   The `openai` library enables seamless integration with OpenAI models.

```bash
---
pip install openai
```

3. **Test the API Connection**
   Create a simple script to verify your setup:

```python
---
import openai

openai.api_key = "your_api_key"

response = openai.Completion.create(
    engine="text-davinci-003",
    prompt="Say hello to Graph RAG!",
    max_tokens=10
)

print(response.choices[0].text.strip())
```

Organize Your Project Structure

A well-structured project keeps your work manageable and organized.
Here's a recommended layout:

```bash
---
project/
│
├── data/                 # Data files (CSV, JSON, etc.)
├── scripts/              # Python scripts for querying and
processing
├── notebooks/            # Jupyter notebooks for
experimentation
├── config/               # Configuration files (API keys,
environment settings)
```

```
└── requirements.txt    # List of dependencies
```

This structure separates data, scripts, and configuration, making collaboration and maintenance easier.

Enable Version Control

Set up Git to track your project's changes:

```bash
---
git init
```

Create a `.gitignore` file to exclude sensitive or unnecessary files:

```
---
config/*.env
__pycache__/
```

Connect your repository to GitHub for remote backup and collaboration:

```bash
---
git remote add origin
https://github.com/your_username/your_project.git
```

Validating the Environment

After setup, validate each component to ensure everything is working smoothly.

1. **Test Neo4j Queries**
   Run a query using Python:

```python
---
from neo4j import GraphDatabase

driver = GraphDatabase.driver("bolt://localhost:7687",
auth=("neo4j", "your_password"))

with driver.session() as session:
```

```
    result = session.run("RETURN 'Neo4j connection
successful!' AS message")
    for record in result:
        print(record["message"])
```

2. **Test OpenAI Integration**
   Use the earlier API test script to confirm successful communication with OpenAI's servers.
3. **Combine Components**
   Write a simple script that queries Neo4j and uses OpenAI to generate a response:

```python
---
# Query Neo4j and format the data for OpenAI
with driver.session() as session:
    result = session.run("MATCH (n) RETURN n.name AS name
LIMIT 1")
    node_name = next(result)["name"]

response = openai.Completion.create(
    engine="text-davinci-003",
    prompt=f"Describe the node: {node_name}",
    max_tokens=50
)
print(response.choices[0].text.strip())
```

Best Practices for Development

- **Automate Setup**: Use tools like `venv` or `conda` for environment isolation and `requirements.txt` for dependency management.
- **Use Environment Variables**: Store sensitive information like API keys in `.env` files and load them using libraries like `python-dotenv`.
- **Set Up Logging**: Implement logging to monitor your application and debug issues efficiently.

Conclusion

Setting up a development environment is an essential step in building Graph RAG pipelines. By carefully configuring your tools and organizing your project, you create a solid foundation for experimentation and growth. With

Neo4j and OpenAI integrated into your environment, you're now ready to dive into building powerful, context-aware applications.

4.2 Popular Graph Databases: Neo4j, Dgraph, and Others

Graph databases are the backbone of modern graph-based systems. They enable efficient storage, retrieval, and analysis of complex, interconnected data. This section introduces some of the most popular graph databases, their strengths, and practical use cases. By the end, you'll have a clearer understanding of which database suits your needs and how to get started with them.

Why Graph Databases?

Traditional relational databases struggle to handle highly interconnected data because their tabular structure requires complex joins to traverse relationships. Graph databases, on the other hand, are designed for relationship-centric data, allowing for efficient traversal and complex queries.

For example, in a healthcare domain, graph databases can model diseases, symptoms, and treatments as nodes and their relationships (e.g., "caused by," "treated with") as edges. Queries like "What are the treatments for Type 2 diabetes?" become natural and efficient.

Neo4j

Neo4j is arguably the most widely used graph database, known for its ease of use and robust feature set. It employs the Cypher query language, which is intuitive and SQL-like, making it accessible for developers transitioning from relational databases.

Key Features

- **User-Friendly Interface**: The Neo4j Browser offers a visual query editor and results visualization.
- **Scalability**: Suitable for small to medium-sized datasets.
- **Rich Ecosystem**: Includes libraries like py2neo for Python integration.

When to Use Neo4j

Neo4j is ideal for applications requiring:

- Knowledge graphs.
- Recommendation systems.
- Fraud detection.

Dgraph

Dgraph is a distributed, horizontally scalable graph database optimized for performance. It uses GraphQL as its query language, making it a favorite among developers familiar with modern web technologies.

Key Features

- **High Performance**: Designed for real-time queries across massive datasets.
- **GraphQL Native**: Simplifies integration with web applications.
- **Horizontal Scalability**: Handles large-scale, distributed systems.

When to Use Dgraph

Dgraph excels in:

- Real-time analytics.
- Applications with a high query throughput.
- Web-based systems using GraphQL.

TigerGraph

TigerGraph focuses on large-scale graph analytics and dynamic graph queries. It's designed for enterprise-grade applications with advanced data processing needs.

Key Features

- **Graph Analytics**: Built-in support for complex analytics like shortest path and community detection.
- **Real-Time Processing**: Handles dynamic data updates and queries efficiently.
- **Enterprise-Ready**: Suited for industries like finance, healthcare, and telecom.

When to Use TigerGraph

TigerGraph is ideal for:

- Real-time fraud detection.
- Supply chain optimization.
- Social network analysis.

Other Noteworthy Graph Databases

Amazon Neptune
A fully managed graph database service in AWS. It supports multiple query languages (Gremlin, SPARQL, openCypher) and integrates seamlessly with other AWS tools.

ArangoDB
A multi-model database supporting graph, document, and key-value stores. It's versatile and a good choice for projects requiring hybrid data models.

OrientDB
A multi-model database with graph capabilities. It offers flexibility for projects combining graph, document, and object-oriented models.

JanusGraph
An open-source graph database optimized for scalability and integration with big data systems. Works well with technologies like Hadoop and Cassandra.

Hands-On with Neo4j

Let's explore how to set up and query a Neo4j database with Python.

Step 1: Install Neo4j

1. Download Neo4j Community Edition from Neo4j's website.
2. Follow the installation instructions for your operating system.
3. Start the database and note the connection details (Bolt URL, username, and password).

Step 2: Install the Required Library

Install the neo4j Python library:

```bash
---
pip install neo4j
```

Step 3: Create a Simple Graph

We'll create a small graph representing diseases, symptoms, and treatments using Cypher queries:

```cypher
---
CREATE (d:Disease {name: "Type 2 Diabetes"})
CREATE (s:Symptom {name: "High Glucose"})
CREATE (t:Treatment {name: "Metformin"})
CREATE (d)-[:HAS_SYMPTOM]->(s)
CREATE (d)-[:TREATED_BY]->(t)
```

Step 4: Query the Graph

Write a Python script to query Neo4j:

```python
---
from neo4j import GraphDatabase

# Connection details
uri = "bolt://localhost:7687"
user = "neo4j"
```

```
password = "your_password"

# Initialize the driver
driver = GraphDatabase.driver(uri, auth=(user, password))

# Query function
def fetch_data():
    query = """
    MATCH (d:Disease)-[:HAS_SYMPTOM]->(s:Symptom),
          (d)-[:TREATED_BY]->(t:Treatment)
    RETURN d.name AS disease, s.name AS symptom, t.name AS
treatment
    """
    with driver.session() as session:
        results = session.run(query)
        for record in results:
            print(f"Disease: {record['disease']}, Symptom:
{record['symptom']}, Treatment: {record['treatment']}")

fetch_data()

# Close the driver
driver.close()
```

Expected Output

```
---
Disease: Type 2 Diabetes, Symptom: High Glucose, Treatment:
Metformin
```

Best Practices

- **Choose the Right Database**: Match the database's features to your project's scale and complexity.
- **Optimize Queries**: Write efficient queries to minimize latency, especially for large graphs.
- **Plan for Scalability**: If your project might grow, consider distributed databases like Dgraph or TigerGraph.

4.3 Libraries for LLMs and RAG Pipelines

Libraries form the foundation of any development project, and when building Retrieval-Augmented Generation (RAG) pipelines with Large

Language Models (LLMs), the right libraries can make all the difference. This section explores essential libraries for working with LLMs and RAG pipelines, highlighting their strengths and providing practical guidance for implementation.

Why Libraries Are Essential for RAG Pipelines

Building a RAG pipeline involves multiple steps: data retrieval, preprocessing, integration with LLMs, and generating meaningful responses. Libraries simplify these tasks by providing robust, pre-built functionalities. They also accelerate development by abstracting complex operations like vector similarity search, embedding generation, and API interactions.

Key Libraries for LLMs and RAG

1. OpenAI Python SDK

The OpenAI library is a go-to choice for working with GPT models like GPT-3 and GPT-4. It provides seamless integration with OpenAI's API, allowing you to generate text, embeddings, and fine-tune models.

- **Strengths**: Easy to use, supports powerful LLMs, and handles tasks like text generation and completion.
- **Best Use Cases**: Natural language understanding, conversational AI, summarization, and RAG pipelines requiring strong generative capabilities.

2. Hugging Face Transformers

Hugging Face offers a treasure trove of pre-trained transformer models for tasks like text generation, question answering, and embedding generation. It supports models like BERT, GPT-2, and T5.

- **Strengths**: Extensive model library, active community, and flexibility for fine-tuning models.

- **Best Use Cases**: Building domain-specific RAG pipelines, embedding-based retrieval, and working offline without relying on APIs.

3. LangChain

LangChain is specifically designed for building applications with LLMs. It provides tools for chaining LLM interactions, handling prompts, and integrating external data sources like vector databases.

- **Strengths**: Streamlines RAG pipeline creation, supports prompt chaining, and integrates well with graph databases and LLM APIs.
- **Best Use Cases**: Complex RAG pipelines, chatbots, and applications requiring multiple steps of reasoning.

4. Haystack

Haystack is an open-source framework tailored for RAG systems. It combines retrieval and generation functionalities, supporting multiple databases and LLMs.

- **Strengths**: Pre-built RAG pipeline components, support for vector search, and integration with libraries like Hugging Face.
- **Best Use Cases**: Rapid prototyping of RAG systems, hybrid search pipelines, and QA systems.

Practical Implementation: Building a Simple RAG Pipeline

Let's create a basic RAG pipeline using OpenAI and LangChain. This example retrieves relevant information from a graph database and uses GPT to generate a response.

Step 1: Install Required Libraries

Install the necessary dependencies:

```bash
---
```

```
pip install openai langchain neo4j
```

Step 2: Query Graph Data

We'll use Neo4j to retrieve relevant context for the user query.

```python
from neo4j import GraphDatabase

# Neo4j connection setup
uri = "bolt://localhost:7687"
username = "neo4j"
password = "your_password"

driver = GraphDatabase.driver(uri, auth=(username, password))

def query_graph(query):
    with driver.session() as session:
        result = session.run(query)
        return [record for record in result]
```

Example query:

```python
graph_query = """
MATCH (d:Disease {name: 'Type 2 Diabetes'})-[:HAS_SYMPTOM]-
>(s:Symptom),
      (d)-[:TREATED_BY]->(t:Treatment)
RETURN d.name AS disease, s.name AS symptom, t.name AS
treatment
"""
data = query_graph(graph_query)
```

Step 3: Process Retrieved Data

Convert graph data into text for the LLM:

```python
def preprocess_data(records):
    sentences = []
    for record in records:
        sentences.append(
```

```
            f"Disease: {record['disease']} is associated with
the symptom {record['symptom']} and is treated with
{record['treatment']}."
        )
    return " ".join(sentences)

context = preprocess_data(data)
```

Step 4: Use LangChain for Prompt Creation

LangChain simplifies prompt creation and chaining for LLMs:

```python
---
from langchain.prompts import PromptTemplate

# Create a LangChain prompt
user_query = "What are the treatments for Type 2 diabetes?"
prompt_template = PromptTemplate(
    input_variables=["query", "context"],
    template="User query: {query}\nContext:
{context}\nAnswer:"
)

prompt = prompt_template.format(query=user_query,
context=context)
```

Step 5: Generate a Response with OpenAI

Send the prompt to OpenAI's API to generate a response:

```python
---
import openai

# OpenAI API setup
openai.api_key = "your_openai_api_key"

response = openai.Completion.create(
    engine="text-davinci-003",
    prompt=prompt,
    max_tokens=150
)

print(response.choices[0].text.strip())
```

Expected Output

The pipeline produces a natural language response based on the graph data. For example:

"Type 2 diabetes is associated with the symptom High Glucose and is treated with Metformin. Metformin is a highly effective first-line treatment."

Comparison of Libraries

Library	Strengths	Use Cases
OpenAI	Powerful LLMs, easy to use API	General-purpose NLP, text generation
Hugging Face	Extensive models, offline capabilities	Domain-specific pipelines
LangChain	RAG-specific tools, chaining capabilities	Complex RAG pipelines
Haystack	Pre-built RAG components	Rapid prototyping, hybrid search

Best Practices for Using Libraries

- **Combine Libraries**: Use LangChain for pipeline orchestration and OpenAI for generative tasks.
- **Optimize Preprocessing**: Ensure the context passed to LLMs is concise and relevant to avoid token overflow.
- **Experiment and Iterate**: Test multiple libraries to find the optimal setup for your use case.

Conclusion

Libraries like OpenAI, Hugging Face, LangChain, and Haystack provide essential building blocks for creating RAG pipelines. By leveraging their strengths and integrating them thoughtfully, you can build systems that efficiently retrieve and generate meaningful responses. This example offers a starting point for exploring the immense possibilities of RAG pipelines.

4.4 Selecting the Right Tools for Your Use Case

Choosing the right tools for a Retrieval-Augmented Generation (RAG) pipeline is a critical step in building an efficient and effective system. With numerous options available for graph databases, LLM frameworks, and RAG libraries, making the right choice requires understanding your use case, project goals, and constraints.

Let's explore how to evaluate and select the best tools for your needs, blending insights with practical advice.

Understanding Your Use Case

Start by clearly defining your project's requirements. A deep understanding of what you need to achieve will help narrow down the toolset.

Ask yourself:

- **What is the scale of my data?** Smaller projects may work well with standalone graph databases like Neo4j, while large-scale systems may need distributed solutions like Dgraph.
- **Do I need real-time performance?** Applications requiring immediate results, like fraud detection or customer support, benefit from tools optimized for low-latency queries.
- **How complex are my queries?** Projects requiring multi-hop reasoning or advanced analytics may require powerful graph databases like TigerGraph.
- **What is my budget?** Free or open-source tools like JanusGraph and Haystack might be better for tight budgets, while enterprise tools like Amazon Neptune offer managed services at a cost.

Matching Tools to Your Use Case

Knowledge Graphs for Research or Education

If you're building a knowledge graph for a focused domain, such as a scientific research assistant or an educational tool, **Neo4j** is an excellent starting point. It offers an intuitive interface, an easy-to-learn Cypher query language, and robust visualization capabilities. Tools like **LangChain** can then be integrated for prompt chaining with LLMs.

Real-Time Decision Systems

For systems that require real-time insights, such as fraud detection or dynamic pricing, **TigerGraph** shines. Its ability to handle large-scale graph analytics in real-time makes it ideal for applications requiring high throughput and low latency.

Large-Scale, Distributed Systems

Projects involving massive datasets, like social network analysis or IoT systems, benefit from the horizontal scalability of **Dgraph**. Its GraphQL-based querying simplifies integration with modern web applications while maintaining high performance.

Semantic Search and Hybrid RAG Pipelines

If your pipeline combines semantic search and LLM-based generation, frameworks like **Haystack** offer a complete solution. Pairing Haystack with **Pinecone** or **FAISS** for vector search ensures a seamless retrieval process.

Offline or Domain-Specific LLM Applications

For use cases requiring domain-specific language models or offline processing, **Hugging Face Transformers** is an excellent choice. It allows fine-tuning of pre-trained models and offers flexibility in deploying models without relying on APIs.

Evaluating Tools Based on Features

When comparing tools, focus on how their features align with your project needs:

Ease of Use For smaller teams or projects with limited development time, prioritize tools with low learning curves. Neo4j's Cypher language, for instance, is easy to pick up, while GraphQL makes Dgraph highly approachable for developers familiar with web APIs.

Scalability If you anticipate significant growth in your dataset or user base, choose tools designed for scalability. Distributed databases like TigerGraph and Dgraph are excellent for handling large-scale applications.

Performance Real-time systems benefit from tools that prioritize speed and efficiency. Evaluate the query performance of graph databases and the latency of LLM APIs to ensure they meet your requirements.

Integration Ensure your tools work well together. LangChain, for example, seamlessly integrates LLMs, vector stores, and graph databases, making it a powerful option for complex pipelines.

Cost Consider your budget. Free and open-source tools like JanusGraph and Haystack offer flexibility without subscription fees, but managed services like Amazon Neptune might save time and resources for cloud-based projects.

Personal Perspective: Lessons Learned

One lesson I've learned from building RAG pipelines is the importance of starting small and scaling as needed. For instance, in a healthcare project, I began with Neo4j to model relationships between diseases, symptoms, and treatments. As the dataset grew, we transitioned to TigerGraph for its scalability and real-time processing capabilities. This phased approach allowed us to manage complexity incrementally without overwhelming the team.

Another insight is that no single tool fits all use cases. Combining tools often yields the best results. For example, pairing Haystack for retrieval with OpenAI's GPT models for generation created a robust system that handled both semantic search and natural language responses efficiently.

Practical Tips for Selection

Run Pilot Tests Before committing to a tool, run a small-scale pilot to evaluate its performance and compatibility with your project. Use sample data and queries to gauge usability and efficiency.

Leverage Community Support Active communities can be a lifesaver during development. Libraries like Hugging Face and Neo4j have vibrant forums and extensive documentation, making it easier to troubleshoot and learn.

Consider Future Needs Think about how your project might evolve. If you plan to expand into multilingual support or integrate additional data sources, ensure your chosen tools can accommodate those changes.

Decision Framework

Use this framework to guide your selection process:

1. **Define Project Goals** Clearly articulate what your pipeline should achieve, including performance, scalability, and complexity.
2. **Prioritize Requirements** Rank the importance of features like ease of use, real-time capabilities, and integration with existing systems.
3. **Evaluate Options** Test a few tools that meet your top priorities, focusing on their strengths and trade-offs.
4. **Plan for Growth** Choose tools that can grow with your project, reducing the need for disruptive migrations later.

Conclusion

Selecting the right tools for your RAG pipeline is about balancing your current needs with future goals. Whether you're building a small-scale knowledge graph with Neo4j, scaling up with TigerGraph, or integrating sophisticated LLMs using LangChain, the key is to align your tools with your use case. By carefully evaluating features, performance, and compatibility, you can create a robust foundation for your Graph RAG pipeline.

Chapter 5: Practical Implementation

Welcome to the heart of building your own Graph-Enhanced RAG (Retrieval-Augmented Generation) application. This chapter is all about translating theory into practice, guiding you through the process of creating a functional Graph RAG system. We'll explore step-by-step instructions, delve into query optimization, handle real-time updates, and culminate with an example project: building a FAQ bot. Let's embark on this hands-on journey together.

5.1 Step-by-Step Guide to Building a Graph RAG Application

Building a Retrieval-Augmented Generation (RAG) application that leverages graph databases and Large Language Models (LLMs) is an exciting journey into creating intelligent, context-aware systems. Whether you're aiming to develop a sophisticated chatbot, a dynamic recommendation engine, or a research assistant, this guide will walk you through the process step-by-step. Drawing from my own experiences, I'll share insights and practical tips to help you navigate each stage with confidence.

Project Overview

Let's embark on building a simple yet powerful Graph RAG application: a **Healthcare FAQ Bot**. This bot will answer user queries about diseases, their symptoms, and available treatments by retrieving relevant information from a knowledge graph and generating coherent responses using an LLM.

Step 1: Define the Scope and Objectives

Before diving into the technical setup, it's crucial to outline what your application will achieve. For our Healthcare FAQ Bot, the objectives are:

- **Answering Questions**: Provide accurate information about diseases, symptoms, and treatments.
- **Contextual Responses**: Ensure responses are contextually relevant and comprehensive.
- **Scalability**: Design the system to handle increasing data and user interactions seamlessly.

Insight: Defining clear objectives from the outset helps in making informed decisions about data modeling, technology selection, and feature prioritization.

Step 2: Design the Knowledge Graph

A well-structured knowledge graph is the foundation of your RAG application. It organizes information in a way that highlights relationships and context.

Entities and Relationships:

- **Entities (Nodes)**: Diseases, Symptoms, Treatments.
- **Relationships (Edges)**: "HAS_SYMPTOM", "TREATED_BY".

For example, the disease "Type 2 Diabetes" **HAS_SYMPTOM** "High Glucose" and is **TREATED_BY** "Metformin".

Insight: Start simple. Focus on core entities and relationships that directly support your application's objectives. This approach keeps the graph manageable and relevant.

Step 3: Set Up Your Graph Database with Neo4j

Neo4j is a user-friendly graph database that's perfect for beginners and robust enough for complex applications.

Installation and Configuration:

1. **Download Neo4j**: Visit the Neo4j website and download the Community Edition or Neo4j Desktop.

2. **Install and Launch**: Follow the installation instructions for your operating system. Once installed, launch Neo4j and create a new project.
3. **Set Credentials**: Note down your Neo4j credentials (username and password) for future use.

Creating the Knowledge Graph: Open the Neo4j Browser and execute the following Cypher queries to create nodes and relationships:

```cypher
---
// Create Disease Nodes
CREATE (d1:Disease {name: "Type 2 Diabetes"})
CREATE (d2:Disease {name: "Hypertension"})

// Create Symptom Nodes
CREATE (s1:Symptom {name: "High Glucose"})
CREATE (s2:Symptom {name: "High Blood Pressure"})

// Create Treatment Nodes
CREATE (t1:Treatment {name: "Metformin"})
CREATE (t2:Treatment {name: "Beta Blockers"})

// Create Relationships
MATCH (d:Disease {name: "Type 2 Diabetes"}), (s:Symptom
{name: "High Glucose"})
CREATE (d)-[:HAS_SYMPTOM]->(s)

MATCH (d:Disease {name: "Type 2 Diabetes"}), (t:Treatment
{name: "Metformin"})
CREATE (d)-[:TREATED_BY]->(t)

MATCH (d:Disease {name: "Hypertension"}), (s:Symptom {name:
"High Blood Pressure"})
CREATE (d)-[:HAS_SYMPTOM]->(s)

MATCH (d:Disease {name: "Hypertension"}), (t:Treatment {name:
"Beta Blockers"})
CREATE (d)-[:TREATED_BY]->(t)
```

Insight: Visualizing the graph in Neo4j Browser helps in understanding the data structure and ensuring that relationships are correctly established.

Step 4: Connect to Neo4j Using Python

To interact with your graph database programmatically, Python is an excellent choice due to its simplicity and the rich ecosystem of libraries.

Install Required Libraries:

```bash
---
pip install neo4j openai pandas
```

Establishing Connection: Here's a Python script to connect to Neo4j and fetch data:

```python
---
from neo4j import GraphDatabase

# Neo4j connection details
URI = "bolt://localhost:7687"
USER = "neo4j"
PASSWORD = "your_password"

# Initialize the Neo4j driver
driver = GraphDatabase.driver(URI, auth=(USER, PASSWORD))

def fetch_data(disease_name):
    query = """
    MATCH (d:Disease {name: $disease_name})-[:HAS_SYMPTOM]-
>(s:Symptom),
          (d)-[:TREATED_BY]->(t:Treatment)
    RETURN d.name AS disease, s.name AS symptom, t.name AS
treatment
    """
    with driver.session() as session:
        result = session.run(query,
disease_name=disease_name)
        return [record for record in result]

# Example usage
data = fetch_data("Type 2 Diabetes")
print(data)

# Close the driver
driver.close()
```

My Experience Testing the connection and basic queries early ensures that your setup is correct and helps identify any configuration issues before moving forward.

Step 5: Preprocess Retrieved Data for the LLM

The data fetched from Neo4j needs to be transformed into a format that the LLM can utilize effectively.

Data Transformation: Convert the structured graph data into natural language sentences that provide context for the LLM.

```python
---
def preprocess_data(records):
    sentences = []
    for record in records:
        disease = record["disease"]
        symptom = record["symptom"]
        treatment = record["treatment"]
        sentences.append(f"{disease} is associated with the
symptom {symptom} and is treated with {treatment}.")
    return " ".join(sentences)

# Preprocess the data
context = preprocess_data(data)
print(context)
```

Insight: Crafting clear and concise sentences from graph data enhances the LLM's ability to generate accurate and relevant responses.

Step 6: Integrate with OpenAI's GPT-4 for Response Generation

With the preprocessed data, you can now leverage GPT-4 to generate natural language responses.

Set Up OpenAI API:

1. **Obtain API Key**: Sign up at OpenAI and get your API key.
2. **Install OpenAI Library**: Ensure the `openai` library is installed (covered in Step 4).

Generating Responses: Here's how to integrate the preprocessed data with GPT-4 to generate responses:

```python
---
import openai

# Set your OpenAI API key
openai.api_key = "your_openai_api_key"

def generate_response(user_query, context):
    prompt = f"User query: {user_query}\nContext:
{context}\nAnswer:"
    response = openai.Completion.create(
        engine="text-davinci-004",
        prompt=prompt,
        max_tokens=150
    )
    return response.choices[0].text.strip()

# Example usage
user_query = "What are the treatments for Type 2 diabetes?"
response = generate_response(user_query, context)
print("Response:", response)
```

Insight: Fine-tuning the prompt by clearly delineating the user query and the context ensures that the LLM generates precise and relevant answers.

Step 7: Develop the User Interface

The final piece is creating an interface through which users can interact with your FAQ bot. This could be a web-based chat interface, a messaging app integration, or even a simple command-line tool.

Web-Based Interface Example: Using Flask, a lightweight web framework, you can create a simple web interface.

```python
---
from flask import Flask, request, jsonify

app = Flask(__name__)

@app.route('/faq', methods=['POST'])
def faq_bot():
    user_query = request.json.get('query')
    data = fetch_data(user_query.split()[-1])  # Simplistic
extraction
    context = preprocess_data(data)
```

```
    answer = generate_response(user_query, context)
    return jsonify({"response": answer})

if __name__ == '__main__':
    app.run(debug=True)
```

Insight: Building a simple interface helps in testing the entire pipeline end-to-end, ensuring that each component interacts seamlessly with the others.

Step 8: Test and Iterate

Thorough testing is essential to ensure your application works as intended. Engage with diverse queries to evaluate the accuracy and relevance of responses.

Testing Tips:

- **Variety of Queries**: Test with different disease names, symptoms, and treatment questions.
- **Edge Cases**: Handle queries with missing or ambiguous information gracefully.
- **Performance**: Assess response times and optimize queries or preprocessing steps if necessary.

Insight: Iterative testing and feedback loops are invaluable. They help identify gaps in the knowledge graph and improve the preprocessing logic, enhancing the overall system's performance.

Conclusion

Building a Graph RAG application involves a harmonious blend of graph databases, data preprocessing, and LLM integration. By following this step-by-step guide, you've laid the groundwork for creating a Healthcare FAQ Bot that retrieves and generates intelligent, context-aware responses. Remember, the key to success lies in a well-structured knowledge graph, efficient data handling, and thoughtful integration of technologies. As you continue to refine your application, you'll uncover deeper insights and unlock new possibilities for intelligent systems.

5.2 Query Optimization with Graph-Based Retrieval

Optimizing queries in a Graph RAG (Retrieval-Augmented Generation) system is akin to fine-tuning an engine—both enhance performance and ensure smooth operations. Efficient query optimization not only accelerates data retrieval but also ensures that the system remains responsive and scalable as your dataset grows. In this section, we'll explore the intricacies of query optimization in graph databases, sharing insights from real-world experiences and providing a practical, step-by-step implementation guide.

Understanding the Importance of Query Optimization

When building a Graph RAG pipeline, the speed and efficiency of data retrieval directly impact the user experience. Slow queries can lead to delays in response generation, frustrating users and diminishing the system's reliability. Moreover, as your knowledge graph expands, maintaining optimal query performance becomes increasingly critical to handle the growing complexity and volume of data.

In my early projects, I noticed that as the graph grew, queries that once ran seamlessly began to lag. This highlighted the necessity of understanding and implementing query optimization techniques to sustain performance and scalability.

Key Concepts in Query Optimization

Before diving into optimization techniques, it's essential to grasp some foundational concepts:

Indexing:
Indexes are like roadmaps for your graph database, allowing it to locate nodes and relationships quickly without scanning the entire graph. Proper indexing can drastically reduce query times, especially for large datasets.

Query Patterns:
The way you structure your queries can significantly impact performance. Efficient query patterns minimize unnecessary traversals and focus on retrieving only the most relevant data.

Caching:
Caching frequently accessed data can reduce the load on your graph database, speeding up response times for common queries.

Profiling and Monitoring:
Regularly profiling your queries helps identify bottlenecks and areas for improvement. Monitoring tools provide insights into query performance, enabling proactive optimization.

Techniques for Optimizing Graph Queries

Optimizing graph queries involves a combination of strategic indexing, refining query patterns, and leveraging caching mechanisms. Let's delve into each technique with practical insights and examples.

1. Strategic Indexing

Creating indexes on frequently queried properties can significantly enhance query performance. In Neo4j, indexing ensures that searches on specific node properties are swift and efficient.

My Experience
In one of my projects, indexing the `name` property of disease nodes transformed query performance. What once took seconds now executed in milliseconds, providing near-instantaneous responses.

Implementation Example:

```cypher
// Creating an index on the 'name' property of Disease nodes
CREATE INDEX disease_name_index FOR (d:Disease) ON (d.name);
```

Step-by-Step Guide:

1. **Identify Frequent Queries:**
   Analyze your most common queries to determine which properties are frequently accessed. For instance, if you often search for diseases by name, indexing the `name` property is crucial.
2. **Create Indexes:**
   Use Cypher to create indexes on these properties. This ensures that Neo4j can quickly locate the relevant nodes without scanning the entire dataset.
3. **Validate Performance Gains:**
   After creating indexes, run your queries again to observe the performance improvements. You should notice a significant reduction in execution time.

2. Refining Query Patterns

Optimizing the structure of your queries can lead to more efficient data retrieval. Avoiding unnecessary traversals and focusing on direct relationships can enhance performance.

My Experience
Initially, my queries were too broad, retrieving excessive data and slowing down the system. By refining them to target specific relationships, I achieved faster and more relevant results.

Implementation Example:

```cypher
---
// Inefficient Query: Retrieves all relationships regardless
of type
MATCH (d:Disease {name: "Type 2 Diabetes"})-[r]->(related)
RETURN d, r, related;

// Optimized Query: Targets specific relationship types
MATCH (d:Disease {name: "Type 2 Diabetes"})-[:HAS_SYMPTOM]-
>(s:Symptom),
      (d)-[:TREATED_BY]->(t:Treatment)
RETURN d.name AS Disease, s.name AS Symptom, t.name AS
Treatment;
```

Step-by-Step Guide:

1. **Analyze Existing Queries:**
   Review your current queries to identify inefficiencies. Look for patterns that retrieve unnecessary nodes or relationships.
2. **Focus on Relevant Relationships:**
   Modify queries to target specific relationship types. This reduces the amount of data processed and speeds up retrieval.
3. **Use Constraints and Filters:**
   Apply constraints within your queries to narrow down the results. For example, specifying node labels and relationship types ensures that only relevant data is fetched.

3. Leveraging Caching Mechanisms

Implementing caching for frequently accessed data can alleviate the load on your graph database, leading to faster response times for repeated queries.

My Experience
In a high-traffic application, caching popular queries dramatically improved user experience by reducing the reliance on real-time database queries.

Implementation Example:

While Neo4j doesn't provide built-in caching for specific queries, integrating an external caching layer like Redis can be effective.

Step-by-Step Guide:

1. **Set Up Redis:**
   Install Redis and configure it as a caching layer for your application.
2. **Implement Caching Logic:**
   Modify your application to check the cache before querying Neo4j. If the data is cached, retrieve it from Redis; otherwise, query Neo4j and store the result in the cache.
3. **Manage Cache Expiry:**
   Set appropriate expiration times for cached data to ensure that the cache remains fresh and relevant.

```python
---
import redis
from neo4j import GraphDatabase

# Initialize Redis
```

```python
cache = redis.Redis(host='localhost', port=6379, db=0)

# Neo4j connection details
driver = GraphDatabase.driver("bolt://localhost:7687",
auth=("neo4j", "password"))

def fetch_data(disease_name):
    # Check cache first
    cached_data = cache.get(disease_name)
    if cached_data:
        return cached_data.decode('utf-8')

    # If not cached, query Neo4j
    query = """
    MATCH (d:Disease {name: $disease_name})-[:HAS_SYMPTOM]-
>(s:Symptom),
          (d)-[:TREATED_BY]->(t:Treatment)
    RETURN d.name AS disease, s.name AS symptom, t.name AS
treatment
    """
    with driver.session() as session:
        result = session.run(query,
disease_name=disease_name)
        data = [f"{record['disease']} is associated with the
symptom {record['symptom']} and is treated with
{record['treatment']}." for record in result]
        context = " ".join(data)
        # Store in cache
        cache.setex(disease_name, 3600, context)  # Expires
in 1 hour
        return context

# Example usage
context = fetch_data("Type 2 Diabetes")
print(context)
```

Profiling and Monitoring Queries

To maintain optimal performance, continuously monitor and profile your queries. Profiling helps you understand how queries execute and where bottlenecks may occur, allowing for informed optimization decisions.

My Experience
Regular profiling revealed that certain multi-hop queries were causing delays. By identifying these bottlenecks, I was able to refine the graph structure and query patterns, leading to substantial performance improvements.

Implementation Example:

Neo4j provides built-in tools for profiling queries, which can be accessed via the Neo4j Browser.

Step-by-Step Guide:

1. **Use the EXPLAIN and PROFILE Commands:**
   - **EXPLAIN:** Shows the execution plan without running the query.
   - **PROFILE:** Executes the query and provides detailed performance metrics.

```cypher
---
PROFILE MATCH (d:Disease {name: "Type 2 Diabetes"})-
[:HAS_SYMPTOM]->(s:Symptom),
                (d)-[:TREATED_BY]->(t:Treatment)
RETURN d.name AS disease, s.name AS symptom, t.name AS
treatment;
```

2. **Analyze the Execution Plan:**

   The execution plan highlights each step of the query, including node lookups, relationship traversals, and return operations. Look for steps that consume the most time or resources.

3. **Identify and Address Bottlenecks:**
   - **High-Cost Operations:** Focus on optimizing steps that have high execution costs.
   - **Unnecessary Traversals:** Eliminate or streamline unnecessary traversals to reduce query complexity.
   - **Index Utilization:** Ensure that your queries are effectively utilizing indexes to speed up data retrieval.
4. **Iterate and Optimize:**

   After making optimizations, re-profile your queries to measure the impact. This iterative process helps you fine-tune your queries for maximum efficiency.

Balancing Read and Write Operations

In dynamic systems, balancing read and write operations is essential to maintain performance and data integrity. Graph databases are optimized for reads, but high write loads can still impact performance if not managed properly.

My Experience

In an application with frequent updates, implementing write batching and optimizing transaction sizes ensured that the graph database remained responsive without compromising data consistency.

Implementation Example:

While Neo4j handles read-heavy workloads exceptionally well, managing write operations requires careful planning.

Step-by-Step Guide:

1. **Batch Writes:**

   Group multiple write operations into a single transaction to reduce overhead and improve throughput.

```python
---
def batch_write(records):
    with driver.session() as session:
        with session.begin_transaction() as tx:
            for record in records:
                tx.run("""
                MERGE (d:Disease {name: $disease})
                MERGE (s:Symptom {name: $symptom})
                MERGE (t:Treatment {name: $treatment})
                MERGE (d)-[:HAS_SYMPTOM]->(s)
                MERGE (d)-[:TREATED_BY]->(t)
                """, disease=record['disease'],
symptom=record['symptom'], treatment=record['treatment'])
            tx.commit()
```

2. **Optimize Transaction Sizes:**

   Avoid overly large transactions that can strain resources. Find a balance that maximizes efficiency without overloading the system.

3. **Use Asynchronous Writes:**

Implement asynchronous processing for write operations to prevent blocking read queries. Libraries like `asyncio` in Python can facilitate this.

Handling Complex Queries with Multi-Hop Reasoning

Multi-hop reasoning involves traversing multiple relationships to derive insights from the graph. Optimizing these complex queries ensures that even intricate data retrieval tasks remain efficient.

My Experience
In a project requiring multi-hop reasoning, optimizing the graph structure to minimize traversal depth and using path length constraints significantly improved query performance without sacrificing the quality of results.

Implementation Example:

Consider a query that not only retrieves treatments for a disease but also finds related research articles cited by those treatments.

Step-by-Step Guide:

1. **Design Efficient Traversals:**

   Limit the number of hops in your query to what's necessary. Excessive traversals can lead to performance issues.

```cypher
---
MATCH (d:Disease {name: "Type 2 Diabetes"})-[:TREATED_BY]-
>(t:Treatment)-[:CITED_IN]->(r:Research)
RETURN t.name AS Treatment, r.title AS ResearchArticle;
```

2. **Use Path Length Constraints:**

   Define maximum path lengths to prevent deep and resource-intensive traversals.

```cypher
---
```

```
MATCH path = (d:Disease {name: "Type 2 Diabetes"})-
[:TREATED_BY*1..2]->(related)
RETURN path;
```

3. **Leverage Aggregations:**

   Aggregate results where possible to reduce the number of individual operations the database must perform.

```cypher
---
MATCH (d:Disease {name: "Type 2 Diabetes"})-[:TREATED_BY]-
>(t:Treatment)
RETURN t.name AS Treatment, COUNT(t) AS TreatmentCount;
```

Personal Perspectives: Lessons from the Field

Throughout my journey in building Graph RAG systems, I've learned that query optimization is both an art and a science. It requires a deep understanding of your data, the relationships within it, and the specific requirements of your application. Here are a few key takeaways:

Start with Simplicity:
Begin with straightforward queries and a well-structured graph. Complexity can be introduced incrementally as you identify performance bottlenecks.

Iterative Optimization:
Optimization is not a one-time task. Continuously profile and refine your queries as your dataset evolves and as new use cases emerge.

Leverage Community Knowledge:
Engage with the graph database community through forums, documentation, and user groups. Sharing experiences and solutions can provide valuable insights and accelerate your optimization efforts.

Embrace Tooling:
Utilize built-in profiling tools and external monitoring solutions to gain visibility into query performance. These tools are indispensable for identifying and addressing inefficiencies.

Conclusion

Query optimization in Graph RAG systems is essential for maintaining high performance, ensuring scalability, and delivering a seamless user experience. By strategically indexing your graph, refining query patterns, leveraging caching, and continuously monitoring performance, you can create efficient and responsive applications. Integrating these optimization techniques not only enhances the speed and reliability of your system but also unlocks the full potential of your knowledge graph, enabling deeper insights and more intelligent responses.

As you apply these principles and techniques, remember that optimization is an ongoing process. Stay curious, keep experimenting, and adapt your strategies as your system grows and evolves. In the next section, we'll explore real-time updates and query handling, ensuring your Graph RAG pipeline remains dynamic and up-to-date.

5.3 Real-Time Updates and Query Handling

In dynamic environments, data is constantly changing. Whether it's new information being added, existing data being updated, or outdated information being removed, a robust Graph RAG (Retrieval-Augmented Generation) system must handle these real-time updates seamlessly. Additionally, efficient query handling ensures that users receive timely and accurate responses. This section delves into strategies for managing real-time updates and optimizing query handling in your Graph RAG pipeline, complemented by a practical implementation guide.

The Importance of Real-Time Updates

Real-time updates are crucial for maintaining the accuracy and relevance of the information your Graph RAG system provides. In applications such as healthcare, finance, or customer support, outdated or incorrect data can lead to poor decision-making and diminished user trust. Ensuring that your knowledge graph reflects the most current data enhances the reliability and effectiveness of your RAG pipeline.

Effective query handling complements real-time updates by ensuring that user queries are processed swiftly and accurately, even as the underlying data evolves. This balance between updating and querying is essential for delivering a responsive and dependable user experience.

Handling Real-Time Data Updates

Managing real-time updates involves efficiently incorporating new data and modifying existing data without disrupting the system's performance. Here are key considerations and steps to handle real-time updates effectively:

Efficient Data Ingestion

To handle real-time updates, your system must support efficient data ingestion mechanisms. This involves:

- **Streaming Data Sources:** Integrate with streaming platforms like Apache Kafka or AWS Kinesis to receive continuous data feeds.
- **Batch Processing:** For periodic updates, implement batch processing to handle bulk data changes without overwhelming the system.
- **API Integrations:** Use APIs to receive updates from external systems, ensuring that new data is promptly reflected in the graph.

Maintaining Data Consistency

Consistency is paramount when updating your graph database. Implementing transactional operations ensures that updates are applied correctly and atomically. This prevents partial updates that could lead to data inconsistencies.

- **Atomic Transactions:** Ensure that each update operation is atomic, meaning it either completes fully or not at all.
- **Validation Rules:** Apply validation rules to verify the integrity of data before it is inserted or updated in the graph.
- **Conflict Resolution:** Implement strategies to handle conflicting updates, especially in distributed systems where multiple sources might modify the same data simultaneously.

Incremental Updates

Rather than reloading the entire dataset with each update, incremental updates allow you to modify only the parts of the graph that have changed. This approach reduces the load on your database and speeds up the update process.

- **Change Detection:** Implement mechanisms to detect changes in data sources and identify the specific nodes and relationships that need updating.
- **Partial Transactions:** Apply updates to specific nodes and edges without affecting the entire graph, ensuring minimal disruption.

Optimizing Query Handling

Efficient query handling ensures that users receive prompt and accurate responses, even as the data grows and changes. Optimization techniques focus on improving query performance and reducing latency.

Indexing for Faster Retrieval

Indexing is a fundamental technique for speeding up query processing. By creating indexes on frequently queried properties, you enable the graph database to locate nodes and relationships quickly without scanning the entire dataset.

- **Property Indexes:** Index properties that are commonly used in search queries, such as `name`, `type`, or `status`.
- **Composite Indexes:** For queries that involve multiple properties, composite indexes can enhance performance by indexing combinations of properties.

Optimizing Query Structures

The way queries are structured can significantly impact their performance. Optimizing query patterns involves:

- **Selective Matching:** Use precise matching criteria to limit the search scope. For example, specifying node labels and relationship types narrows down the traversal paths.
- **Limiting Traversals:** Restrict the number of hops in multi-hop queries to prevent unnecessary data retrieval.

- **Using Constraints:** Apply constraints within queries to filter results early in the execution process, reducing the amount of data processed.

Caching Frequently Accessed Data

Caching can greatly reduce query response times by storing the results of frequent queries and serving them without hitting the database each time.

- **In-Memory Caching:** Use in-memory caches like Redis or Memcached to store frequently accessed query results.
- **Application-Level Caching:** Implement caching within your application logic to store and retrieve query results as needed.

Load Balancing and Parallel Processing

Distribute query loads across multiple database instances or shards to prevent bottlenecks and ensure that the system remains responsive under high traffic.

- **Horizontal Scaling:** Scale your graph database horizontally by adding more nodes to handle increased query loads.
- **Parallel Query Execution:** Execute multiple queries in parallel to take advantage of multi-core processing capabilities.

Practical Implementation: Real-Time Updates and Optimized Queries

To illustrate how real-time updates and query optimization can be implemented, let's walk through a practical example using Neo4j and Redis for caching.

Step 1: Set Up Redis for Caching

Redis is an in-memory data store that can be used to cache frequently accessed query results.

1. **Install Redis:**
   Follow the installation instructions from the official Redis website.

2. **Start Redis Server:**
   Launch the Redis server on your local machine or configure it on a cloud service.

Step 2: Update Neo4j Connection and Integrate Redis

Extend your existing Neo4j connection to include caching with Redis.

```python
---
import redis
from neo4j import GraphDatabase

# Neo4j connection details
NEO4J_URI = "bolt://localhost:7687"
NEO4J_USER = "neo4j"
NEO4J_PASSWORD = "your_password"

# Initialize Neo4j driver
driver = GraphDatabase.driver(NEO4J_URI, auth=(NEO4J_USER,
NEO4J_PASSWORD))

# Initialize Redis client
cache = redis.Redis(host='localhost', port=6379, db=0)

def fetch_data_with_cache(disease_name):
    # Check if result is in cache
    cached_result = cache.get(disease_name)
    if cached_result:
        return cached_result.decode('utf-8')

    # If not in cache, query Neo4j
    query = """
    MATCH (d:Disease {name: $disease_name})-[:HAS_SYMPTOM]-
>(s:Symptom),
          (d)-[:TREATED_BY]->(t:Treatment)
    RETURN d.name AS disease, s.name AS symptom, t.name AS
treatment
    """
    with driver.session() as session:
        result = session.run(query,
disease_name=disease_name)
        data = [record for record in result]

    # Preprocess data
    context = preprocess_data(data)

    # Store result in cache with an expiration time (e.g., 1
hour)
```

```python
    cache.setex(disease_name, 3600, context)

    return context

def preprocess_data(records):
    sentences = []
    for record in records:
        disease = record["disease"]
        symptom = record["symptom"]
        treatment = record["treatment"]
        sentences.append(f"{disease} is associated with the
symptom {symptom} and is treated with {treatment}.")
    return " ".join(sentences)
```

Step 3: Implement Real-Time Data Updates

To handle real-time updates, create functions that allow adding or modifying nodes and relationships in Neo4j.

```python
---
def add_disease(disease_name):
    query = """
    MERGE (d:Disease {name: $disease_name})
    """
    with driver.session() as session:
        session.run(query, disease_name=disease_name)

def add_symptom(disease_name, symptom_name):
    query = """
    MATCH (d:Disease {name: $disease_name})
    MERGE (s:Symptom {name: $symptom_name})
    MERGE (d)-[:HAS_SYMPTOM]->(s)
    """
    with driver.session() as session:
        session.run(query, disease_name=disease_name,
symptom_name=symptom_name)

def add_treatment(disease_name, treatment_name):
    query = """
    MATCH (d:Disease {name: $disease_name})
    MERGE (t:Treatment {name: $treatment_name})
    MERGE (d)-[:TREATED_BY]->(t)
    """
    with driver.session() as session:
        session.run(query, disease_name=disease_name,
treatment_name=treatment_name)
```

Step 4: Integrate Updates with the Application

Ensure that when new data is added or existing data is updated, the cache is appropriately invalidated or updated to maintain consistency.

```python
---
def update_disease_info(disease_name, symptom_name=None,
treatment_name=None):
    add_disease(disease_name)
    if symptom_name:
        add_symptom(disease_name, symptom_name)
    if treatment_name:
        add_treatment(disease_name, treatment_name)

    # Invalidate cache for the updated disease
    cache.delete(disease_name)

# Example usage
update_disease_info("Type 2 Diabetes", "Increased Thirst",
"Lifestyle Changes")
```

Step 5: Optimize Queries with Indexing

Create indexes on frequently queried properties to enhance query performance.

```python
---
def create_indexes():
    queries = [
        "CREATE INDEX disease_name_index FOR (d:Disease) ON
(d.name)",
        "CREATE INDEX symptom_name_index FOR (s:Symptom) ON
(s.name)",
        "CREATE INDEX treatment_name_index FOR (t:Treatment)
ON (t.name)"
    ]
    with driver.session() as session:
        for query in queries:
            session.run(query)

# Create indexes
create_indexes()
```

Best Practices for Real-Time Updates and Query Handling

- **Efficient Data Ingestion:**
  Use streaming platforms or APIs to handle continuous data updates without overloading the system.
- **Indexing Strategy:**
  Index properties that are frequently used in queries to speed up data retrieval.
- **Cache Management:**
  Implement smart caching strategies that balance between performance and data freshness. Use appropriate expiration times to ensure the cache remains up-to-date.
- **Transaction Management:**
  Handle data updates within transactions to maintain data integrity and consistency.
- **Monitoring and Profiling:**
  Continuously monitor query performance and system health. Use profiling tools to identify and address performance bottlenecks.
- **Scalability Considerations:**
  Design your system to scale horizontally, allowing you to add more resources as your data and user base grow.

Conclusion

Managing real-time updates and optimizing query handling are essential for maintaining the performance and reliability of your Graph RAG pipeline. By implementing efficient data ingestion mechanisms, maintaining data consistency, and optimizing your queries through indexing and caching, you ensure that your system remains responsive and accurate as it scales. Practical implementation steps, such as integrating Redis for caching and creating optimized Cypher queries, provide a solid foundation for building a robust and efficient Graph RAG application.

As you continue to develop and refine your system, keep these optimization strategies in mind to sustain high performance and deliver a seamless user experience. The next section will guide you through building a comprehensive example project—a FAQ bot—demonstrating how to apply these principles in a real-world application.

5.3 Real-Time Updates and Query Handling

In a dynamic environment, data is constantly evolving. Whether it's new information being added, existing data being updated, or outdated information being removed, a Graph RAG (Retrieval-Augmented Generation) system must handle these real-time changes seamlessly. Additionally, efficient query handling ensures that users receive timely and accurate responses. This section explores strategies for managing real-time updates and optimizing query handling in your Graph RAG pipeline, complemented by a practical implementation guide.

The Necessity of Real-Time Updates

Real-time updates are essential for maintaining the accuracy and relevance of the information your Graph RAG system provides. In applications such as healthcare, finance, or customer support, outdated or incorrect data can lead to poor decision-making and diminished user trust. Ensuring that your knowledge graph reflects the most current data enhances the reliability and effectiveness of your RAG pipeline.

Efficient query handling complements real-time updates by ensuring that user queries are processed swiftly and accurately, even as the underlying data evolves. This balance between updating and querying is crucial for delivering a responsive and dependable user experience.

Managing Real-Time Data Updates

Handling real-time updates involves efficiently incorporating new data and modifying existing data without disrupting the system's performance. Here are key strategies to manage real-time updates effectively:

Efficient Data Ingestion

To handle real-time updates, your system must support efficient data ingestion mechanisms. Integrating streaming platforms like Apache Kafka or AWS Kinesis allows your application to receive continuous data feeds. For periodic updates, implementing batch processing can manage bulk data changes without overwhelming the system. Additionally, using APIs to receive updates from external systems ensures that new data is promptly reflected in the graph.

Maintaining Data Consistency

Consistency is paramount when updating your graph database. Implementing transactional operations ensures that updates are applied correctly and atomically, preventing partial updates that could lead to data inconsistencies. Utilizing atomic transactions, applying validation rules to verify data integrity before insertion or modification, and developing conflict resolution strategies are essential practices for maintaining consistency, especially in distributed systems where multiple sources might modify the same data simultaneously.

Incremental Updates

Rather than reloading the entire dataset with each update, incremental updates modify only the parts of the graph that have changed. This approach reduces the load on your database and speeds up the update process. Implementing change detection mechanisms to identify specific nodes and relationships that need updating and applying partial transactions ensures minimal disruption to the system.

Optimizing Query Handling

Efficient query handling ensures that users receive prompt and accurate responses, even as the data grows and changes. Optimization techniques focus on improving query performance and reducing latency.

Indexing for Faster Retrieval

Creating indexes on frequently queried properties can significantly enhance query performance. Indexes act like roadmaps, allowing the graph database to locate nodes and relationships quickly without scanning the entire dataset. By indexing properties commonly used in search queries, such as `name`, `type`, or `status`, you enable the database to execute queries more efficiently.

Optimizing Query Structures

The structure of your queries can greatly impact their performance. Writing efficient query patterns minimizes unnecessary traversals and focuses on retrieving only the most relevant data. By using selective matching criteria, specifying node labels and relationship types, and limiting the number of hops in multi-hop queries, you can streamline data retrieval processes and reduce query complexity.

Caching Frequently Accessed Data

Implementing caching mechanisms for frequently accessed data can alleviate the load on your graph database, leading to faster response times for common queries. Using in-memory caches like Redis or Memcached to store query results allows your application to serve repeated queries quickly without hitting the database each time.

Load Balancing and Parallel Processing

Distributing query loads across multiple database instances or shards helps prevent bottlenecks and ensures that the system remains responsive under high traffic. Horizontal scaling by adding more nodes and executing multiple queries in parallel can leverage multi-core processing capabilities, enhancing overall system performance.

Practical Implementation: Real-Time Updates and Optimized Queries

To illustrate how real-time updates and query optimization can be implemented, let's walk through a practical example using Neo4j and Redis for caching.

Setting Up Redis for Caching

Redis is an in-memory data store that can be used to cache frequently accessed query results, reducing the need for repeated database hits.

1. **Install Redis:**
   Download and install Redis from the official Redis website. Follow the installation instructions for your operating system.

2. **Start Redis Server:**
   Launch the Redis server on your local machine or configure it on a cloud service. Ensure it's running and accessible.

Integrating Redis with Neo4j in Python

Extend your existing Neo4j connection to include caching with Redis, enabling efficient data retrieval and storage.

```python
---
import redis
from neo4j import GraphDatabase

# Neo4j connection details
NEO4J_URI = "bolt://localhost:7687"
NEO4J_USER = "neo4j"
NEO4J_PASSWORD = "your_password"

# Initialize Neo4j driver
driver = GraphDatabase.driver(NEO4J_URI, auth=(NEO4J_USER,
NEO4J_PASSWORD))

# Initialize Redis client
cache = redis.Redis(host='localhost', port=6379, db=0)

def preprocess_data(records):
    sentences = []
    for record in records:
        disease = record["disease"]
        symptom = record["symptom"]
        treatment = record["treatment"]
        sentences.append(f"{disease} is associated with the
symptom {symptom} and is treated with {treatment}.")
    return " ".join(sentences)

def fetch_data_with_cache(disease_name):
    # Check if result is in cache
    cached_result = cache.get(disease_name)
    if cached_result:
        return cached_result.decode('utf-8')

    # If not in cache, query Neo4j
    query = """
    MATCH (d:Disease {name: $disease_name})-[:HAS_SYMPTOM]-
>(s:Symptom),
          (d)-[:TREATED_BY]->(t:Treatment)
    RETURN d.name AS disease, s.name AS symptom, t.name AS
treatment
```

```
    """
    with driver.session() as session:
        result = session.run(query,
disease_name=disease_name)
        data = [record for record in result]

    # Preprocess data
    context = preprocess_data(data)

    # Store result in cache with an expiration time (e.g., 1
hour)
    cache.setex(disease_name, 3600, context)

    return context
```

Implementing Real-Time Data Updates

Create functions to add or modify nodes and relationships in Neo4j, ensuring that the cache is appropriately invalidated or updated to maintain consistency.

```python
---
def add_disease(disease_name):
    query = """
    MERGE (d:Disease {name: $disease_name})
    """
    with driver.session() as session:
        session.run(query, disease_name=disease_name)

def add_symptom(disease_name, symptom_name):
    query = """
    MATCH (d:Disease {name: $disease_name})
    MERGE (s:Symptom {name: $symptom_name})
    MERGE (d)-[:HAS_SYMPTOM]->(s)
    """
    with driver.session() as session:
        session.run(query, disease_name=disease_name,
symptom_name=symptom_name)

def add_treatment(disease_name, treatment_name):
    query = """
    MATCH (d:Disease {name: $disease_name})
    MERGE (t:Treatment {name: $treatment_name})
    MERGE (d)-[:TREATED_BY]->(t)
    """
    with driver.session() as session:
        session.run(query, disease_name=disease_name,
treatment_name=treatment_name)
```

```
def update_disease_info(disease_name, symptom_name=None,
treatment_name=None):
    add_disease(disease_name)
    if symptom_name:
        add_symptom(disease_name, symptom_name)
    if treatment_name:
        add_treatment(disease_name, treatment_name)

    # Invalidate cache for the updated disease
    cache.delete(disease_name)
```

Creating Indexes for Query Optimization

Creating indexes on frequently queried properties enhances query performance by allowing the database to locate nodes quickly.

```python
---
def create_indexes():
    queries = [
        "CREATE INDEX disease_name_index FOR (d:Disease) ON
(d.name)",
        "CREATE INDEX symptom_name_index FOR (s:Symptom) ON
(s.name)",
        "CREATE INDEX treatment_name_index FOR (t:Treatment)
ON (t.name)"
    ]
    with driver.session() as session:
        for query in queries:
            session.run(query)

# Create indexes
create_indexes()
```

Putting It All Together

Here's how the complete implementation works:

1. **Fetching Data with Caching:**
   When a query is made for a disease, the system first checks if the result is cached in Redis. If it is, the cached result is returned immediately. If not, the system queries Neo4j, processes the data, stores the result in Redis for future use, and then returns the context.
2. **Handling Real-Time Updates:**
   When new information is added or existing data is updated, the corresponding functions modify the graph in Neo4j and invalidate the

cache to ensure that future queries retrieve the most up-to-date information.

3. **Optimizing Queries with Indexes:**
   Indexes are created on key properties to ensure that queries run efficiently, even as the dataset grows.

```python
---
# Example Usage
if __name__ == "__main__":
    # Create indexes
    create_indexes()

    # Add new data
    update_disease_info("Type 2 Diabetes",
symptom_name="Increased Thirst", treatment_name="Lifestyle
Changes")

    # Fetch data with caching
    context = fetch_data_with_cache("Type 2 Diabetes")
    print(context)

    # Close the Neo4j driver
    driver.close()
```

Running this script will:

1. Ensure that indexes are created for optimized query performance.
2. Add new symptom and treatment information for "Type 2 Diabetes" and invalidate the cache.
3. Fetch the updated data, which will be retrieved from Neo4j, processed, cached, and then printed.

Best Practices for Real-Time Updates and Query Handling

Maintaining an efficient and responsive Graph RAG system involves adhering to best practices that ensure data integrity, optimize performance, and provide a seamless user experience.

- **Efficient Data Ingestion:**
  Utilize streaming platforms or APIs to handle continuous data updates without overloading the system. Ensure that data flows smoothly from sources to your graph database.

- **Indexing Strategy:**
  Index properties that are frequently used in queries to speed up data retrieval. Consider both single-property and composite indexes based on your query patterns.
- **Cache Management:**
  Implement smart caching strategies that balance performance and data freshness. Use appropriate expiration times to keep the cache updated without unnecessary staleness.
- **Transaction Management:**
  Handle data updates within transactions to maintain data integrity and consistency. Ensure that updates are atomic to prevent partial changes.
- **Monitoring and Profiling:**
  Continuously monitor query performance and system health. Use profiling tools to identify and address performance bottlenecks proactively.
- **Scalability Considerations:**
  Design your system to scale horizontally, allowing you to add more resources as your data and user base grow. This ensures that your application remains responsive under increasing loads.

Conclusion

Managing real-time updates and optimizing query handling are essential for maintaining the performance and reliability of your Graph RAG pipeline. By implementing efficient data ingestion mechanisms, maintaining data consistency, and optimizing your queries through indexing and caching, you ensure that your system remains responsive and accurate as it scales. Practical implementation steps, such as integrating Redis for caching and creating optimized Cypher queries, provide a solid foundation for building a robust and efficient Graph RAG application.

As you continue to develop and refine your system, these strategies will help sustain high performance and deliver a seamless user experience. The next section will guide you through building a comprehensive example project—a FAQ bot—demonstrating how to apply these principles in a real-world application.

Chapter 6: Advanced Techniques

As you delve deeper into building sophisticated Graph RAG (Retrieval-Augmented Generation) systems, advanced techniques become essential for enhancing performance, scalability, and the overall intelligence of your applications. This chapter explores cutting-edge methods, including graph embeddings, semantic search, automated knowledge graph construction, fine-tuning Large Language Models (LLMs) for graph-based tasks, and strategies for scaling Graph RAG pipelines to handle large datasets. These techniques will empower you to create more efficient, intelligent, and scalable systems.

6.1 Graph Embeddings and Semantic Search

Graph embeddings and semantic search are pivotal in enhancing the intelligence and efficiency of Graph RAG (Retrieval-Augmented Generation) systems. By transforming graph-structured data into continuous vector spaces, embeddings facilitate advanced search capabilities that understand context and meaning, rather than relying solely on keyword matching. This section delves into the concepts of graph embeddings and semantic search, explores their significance, and provides a practical implementation guide to integrate these techniques into your Graph RAG pipeline.

Understanding Graph Embeddings

Graph embeddings convert nodes, edges, or entire subgraphs into dense numerical vectors while preserving the graph's structural and semantic properties. These embeddings capture the relationships and patterns within the graph, enabling machine learning models to perform tasks such as classification, clustering, and similarity searches with enhanced accuracy.

Why Graph Embeddings Matter

Traditional graph queries can retrieve relevant nodes and relationships, but they lack the ability to quantify the similarity or relevance between different entities in a nuanced manner. Graph embeddings bridge this gap by representing graph elements in a vector space where geometric relationships reflect semantic similarities. This transformation allows for more sophisticated operations, such as:

- **Similarity Search:** Identifying nodes that are semantically similar based on their embeddings.
- **Clustering:** Grouping nodes with similar characteristics.
- **Classification:** Assigning labels to nodes based on their embeddings.

Types of Graph Embeddings

Several techniques exist to generate graph embeddings, each with its unique approach to capturing graph properties:

- **Node2Vec:** Uses random walks to explore neighborhoods of nodes, capturing local and global structural information.
- **Graph Convolutional Networks (GCNs):** Apply convolution operations on graphs to aggregate and transform node features.
- **Graph Attention Networks (GATs):** Introduce attention mechanisms to weigh the importance of different neighbors during aggregation.
- **DeepWalk:** Similar to Node2Vec, it uses random walks to learn embeddings by treating walks as sentences in natural language processing.

Semantic Search Enhanced by Graph Embeddings

Semantic search leverages the rich information captured by graph embeddings to understand the intent and context behind user queries. Unlike traditional keyword-based search, semantic search interprets the meaning of queries, enabling the retrieval of more relevant and contextually appropriate results.

How Semantic Search Works with Graph Embeddings

1. **Query Embedding:** The user's query is transformed into a vector using the same embedding technique applied to the graph data.
2. **Similarity Measurement:** The system computes the similarity between the query embedding and the embeddings of graph entities.

3. **Relevant Retrieval:** Entities with high similarity scores are retrieved and presented as search results.

This process ensures that the search results are not only relevant based on keywords but also align with the underlying semantics and relationships within the graph.

Practical Implementation: Building Graph Embeddings and Enabling Semantic Search

To illustrate the application of graph embeddings and semantic search, we'll walk through a step-by-step implementation using Python, Neo4j, and the Node2Vec algorithm. This example demonstrates how to generate embeddings for graph nodes and perform semantic search based on these embeddings.

Step 1: Setting Up the Environment

Ensure you have the necessary tools and libraries installed. You'll need Neo4j for managing the graph database, Python for scripting, and the `node2vec` library for generating embeddings.

```bash
---
pip install neo4j node2vec pandas numpy scikit-learn
```

Step 2: Connect to Neo4j and Extract the Graph

Establish a connection to your Neo4j database and extract the graph data needed for embedding generation.

```python
---
from neo4j import GraphDatabase
import pandas as pd

# Neo4j connection details
NEO4J_URI = "bolt://localhost:7687"
NEO4J_USER = "neo4j"
NEO4J_PASSWORD = "your_password"

# Initialize the Neo4j driver
```

```
driver = GraphDatabase.driver(NEO4J_URI, auth=(NEO4J_USER,
NEO4J_PASSWORD))

def get_edges():
    query = """
    MATCH (n)-[r]->(m)
    RETURN n.name AS source, m.name AS target
    """
    with driver.session() as session:
        result = session.run(query)
        edges = pd.DataFrame([record.data() for record in
result])
    return edges

edges = get_edges()
print(edges.head())

# Close the driver
driver.close()
```

Step 3: Generate Graph Embeddings Using Node2Vec

Utilize the `node2vec` library to create embeddings for each node in the graph. These embeddings will capture the structural and semantic relationships between nodes.

```python
---
from node2vec import Node2Vec
import networkx as nx

# Create a NetworkX graph from the edges
G = nx.from_pandas_edgelist(edges, 'source', 'target')

# Initialize and fit Node2Vec
node2vec = Node2Vec(G, dimensions=64, walk_length=30,
num_walks=200, workers=4)
model = node2vec.fit(window=10, min_count=1, batch_words=4)

# Save embeddings for future use
model.wv.save_word2vec_format("node_embeddings.txt")
```

Step 4: Load and Utilize Embeddings for Semantic Search

With the embeddings generated, you can now perform semantic searches by comparing the similarity between query embeddings and node embeddings.

```python
```

```
---
from sklearn.metrics.pairwise import cosine_similarity
import numpy as np

# Load embeddings
from gensim.models import KeyedVectors
embeddings =
KeyedVectors.load_word2vec_format("node_embeddings.txt")

def get_similarity(query, embeddings, top_n=5):
    if query not in embeddings:
        print(f"'{query}' not found in embeddings.")
        return []

    query_vector = embeddings[query].reshape(1, -1)
    all_vectors = embeddings.vectors
    all_names = embeddings.index_to_key
    similarities = cosine_similarity(query_vector,
all_vectors).flatten()

    # Get top N similar nodes
    top_indices = similarities.argsort()[-top_n-1:-1][::-1]
    similar_nodes = [(all_names[i], similarities[i]) for i in
top_indices]
    return similar_nodes

# Example query
query = "Type 2 Diabetes"
similar_nodes = get_similarity(query, embeddings, top_n=3)
print(f"Top similar nodes to '{query}':")
for node, score in similar_nodes:
    print(f"{node}: {score:.4f}")
```

Step 5: Integrate Semantic Search into Your Application

Incorporate the semantic search functionality into your Graph RAG pipeline
to enhance the retrieval process. When a user submits a query, convert it into
an embedding, find similar nodes, and retrieve relevant information from the
graph.

```python
---
def semantic_search(query, embeddings, top_n=5):
    similar_nodes = get_similarity(query, embeddings, top_n)
    if not similar_nodes:
        return "No relevant information found."

    # Connect to Neo4j to retrieve detailed information about
similar nodes
```

```python
    driver = GraphDatabase.driver(NEO4J_URI,
auth=(NEO4J_USER, NEO4J_PASSWORD))

    results = []
    for node, score in similar_nodes:
        query = """
        MATCH (n {name: $node_name})-[:HAS_SYMPTOM]-
>(s:Symptom),
                (n)-[:TREATED_BY]->(t:Treatment)
        RETURN n.name AS disease, s.name AS symptom, t.name
AS treatment
        """
        with driver.session() as session:
            result = session.run(query, node_name=node)
            record = result.single()
            if record:
                results.append({
                    "disease": record["disease"],
                    "symptom": record["symptom"],
                    "treatment": record["treatment"],
                    "similarity_score": score
                })
    driver.close()
    return results

# Example usage
search_results = semantic_search("Type 2 Diabetes",
embeddings, top_n=3)
for result in search_results:
    print(result)
```

Best Practices for Graph Embeddings and Semantic Search

- **Choose the Right Embedding Technique:** Select an embedding method that aligns with your data structure and the specific requirements of your application. Node2Vec is suitable for capturing neighborhood structures, while GCNs are ideal for leveraging node features.
- **Dimensionality Selection:** Balance the dimensionality of embeddings to ensure they are rich enough to capture complex relationships without being computationally expensive.
- **Regular Updates:** As your knowledge graph evolves, regularly update the embeddings to reflect new relationships and entities, ensuring that semantic search remains accurate.

- **Evaluation and Validation:** Continuously evaluate the quality of embeddings by assessing their performance in downstream tasks like search accuracy, clustering, and classification.
- **Scalability Considerations:** For large graphs, consider scalable embedding techniques and distributed processing to handle the computational load efficiently.

Conclusion

Graph embeddings and semantic search are integral components in elevating the capabilities of Graph RAG systems. By transforming graph data into meaningful vector representations, embeddings enable nuanced understanding and retrieval of information based on context and relationships. Integrating these techniques into your pipeline enhances the accuracy and relevance of responses, ensuring that users receive information that truly matches their queries.

6.2 Automating Knowledge Graph Construction

Constructing a knowledge graph manually can be labor-intensive and prone to human error, especially as the volume of data increases. Automating the construction process not only accelerates development but also ensures consistency, scalability, and accuracy. This section explores the methodologies and tools used to automate knowledge graph construction, providing a practical implementation guide to help you build and maintain robust knowledge graphs efficiently.

The Need for Automation in Knowledge Graph Construction

Knowledge graphs serve as structured representations of information, capturing entities and their interrelationships within a specific domain. As data sources grow in volume and complexity, manually curating these graphs becomes impractical. Automation addresses these challenges by streamlining data ingestion, entity recognition, relationship extraction, and integration from diverse sources. This ensures that knowledge graphs remain up-to-date, comprehensive, and reliable without the extensive manual effort traditionally required.

Techniques for Automating Knowledge Graph Construction

Automating knowledge graph construction involves several key processes: data ingestion, entity recognition, relationship extraction, data integration, and validation. Leveraging machine learning and natural language processing (NLP) techniques enhances the accuracy and efficiency of these processes.

Data Ingestion

Data ingestion is the first step, where information from various sources is collected and prepared for processing. Automated pipelines can integrate data from structured sources like databases and unstructured sources like text documents, APIs, and web scraping.

Entity Recognition and Linking

Entity recognition involves identifying and classifying key entities (such as people, organizations, locations, etc.) within unstructured data. Linking these entities to standardized identifiers ensures consistency and facilitates integration across different datasets.

Relationship Extraction

Once entities are identified, the next step is to determine the relationships between them. This involves parsing sentences to understand how entities interact, such as "is a treatment for" or "causes."

Data Integration and Ontology Alignment

Integrating data from multiple sources requires aligning different schemas and ontologies. Automated tools can map disparate data structures into a unified knowledge graph schema, ensuring coherence and interoperability.

Validation and Quality Assurance

Automated validation checks ensure that the constructed knowledge graph maintains data integrity and accuracy. Techniques like consistency checking, anomaly detection, and manual review (where necessary) help maintain high-quality knowledge graphs.

Tools and Frameworks for Automated Knowledge Graph Construction

Several tools and frameworks facilitate the automation of knowledge graph construction, each offering unique features tailored to different aspects of the process.

Natural Language Processing (NLP) Libraries

NLP libraries like **spaCy**, **Stanford NLP**, and **Hugging Face Transformers** provide robust capabilities for entity recognition and relationship extraction from unstructured text.

Information Extraction Tools

Tools such as **Stanford OpenIE** and **Apache OpenNLP** are designed to extract structured information from unstructured data, simplifying the process of identifying entities and their relationships.

Knowledge Graph Platforms

Platforms like **Neo4j** offer comprehensive tools for building, managing, and querying knowledge graphs. Neo4j's **Graph Data Science Library** provides algorithms for data integration, relationship extraction, and graph analytics.

ETL (Extract, Transform, Load) Tools

ETL tools like **Apache NiFi** and **Talend** facilitate the automated ingestion and transformation of data from various sources into the knowledge graph.

Practical Implementation: Automating Knowledge Graph Construction with Python and Neo4j

To demonstrate the automation of knowledge graph construction, let's walk through a practical example using Python, spaCy for NLP, and Neo4j as the graph database. This example will show how to extract entities and relationships from unstructured text and populate a Neo4j knowledge graph automatically.

Step 1: Setting Up the Environment

Ensure you have Python installed along with the necessary libraries. You'll also need a running instance of Neo4j.

```bash
---
pip install spacy neo4j
python -m spacy download en_core_web_sm
```

Step 2: Initialize Neo4j

1. **Download and Install Neo4j**: Visit the Neo4j website and download the Community Edition or Neo4j Desktop. Follow the installation instructions for your operating system.
2. **Start Neo4j**: Launch Neo4j and create a new database. Note the connection details, including the Bolt URL (e.g., `bolt://localhost:7687`), username, and password.

Step 3: Connect to Neo4j Using Python

Establish a connection to your Neo4j database using the `neo4j` Python driver.

```python
---
from neo4j import GraphDatabase

# Neo4j connection details
NEO4J_URI = "bolt://localhost:7687"
NEO4J_USER = "neo4j"
NEO4J_PASSWORD = "your_password"

# Initialize the Neo4j driver
driver = GraphDatabase.driver(NEO4J_URI, auth=(NEO4J_USER, NEO4J_PASSWORD))
```

Step 4: Extract Entities and Relationships Using spaCy

Use spaCy to perform Named Entity Recognition (NER) and extract relationships from unstructured text.

```python
---
import spacy

# Load spaCy's English model
nlp = spacy.load("en_core_web_sm")

def extract_entities_relationships(text):
    doc = nlp(text)
    entities = [(ent.text, ent.label_) for ent in doc.ents]

    relationships = []
    for sent in doc.sents:
        # Simple rule-based relationship extraction
        if 'treated by' in sent.text:
            parts = sent.text.split('treated by')
            if len(parts) == 2:
                disease = parts[0].strip()
                treatment = parts[1].strip().rstrip('.')
                relationships.append((disease, 'TREATED_BY', treatment))
        elif 'caused by' in sent.text:
            parts = sent.text.split('caused by')
            if len(parts) == 2:
                disease = parts[0].strip()
                cause = parts[1].strip().rstrip('.')
                relationships.append((disease, 'CAUSED_BY', cause))
    return entities, relationships
```

Explanation:

- **Entity Extraction:** The `extract_entities_relationships` function uses spaCy to identify entities within the text.
- **Relationship Extraction:** It employs simple rule-based methods to identify relationships like "treated by" and "caused by."

Step 5: Populate the Knowledge Graph in Neo4j

Create nodes and relationships in Neo4j based on the extracted entities and relationships.

```python
---
```

```python
def populate_graph(entities, relationships):
    with driver.session() as session:
        for entity, label in entities:
            # Create nodes based on entity type
            if label == "DISEASE":
                session.run("MERGE (d:Disease {name:
$name})", name=entity)
            elif label == "SYMPTOM":
                session.run("MERGE (s:Symptom {name:
$name})", name=entity)
            elif label == "DRUG":
                session.run("MERGE (t:Treatment {name:
$name})", name=entity)

        for source, relation, target in relationships:
            if relation == 'TREATED_BY':
                session.run("""
                    MATCH (d:Disease {name: $disease}),
(t:Treatment {name: $treatment})
                    MERGE (d)-[:TREATED_BY]->(t)
                """, disease=source, treatment=target)
            elif relation == 'CAUSED_BY':
                session.run("""
                    MATCH (d:Disease {name: $disease}),
(c:Cause {name: $cause})
                    MERGE (d)-[:CAUSED_BY]->(c)
                """, disease=source, cause=target)
```

Explanation:

- **Node Creation:** Depending on the entity type (Disease, Symptom, Treatment), appropriate nodes are created using the MERGE clause to avoid duplicates.
- **Relationship Creation:** Based on the extracted relationships, edges are established between nodes.

Step 6: Automate the Knowledge Graph Construction Process

Combine the extraction and population steps into an automated pipeline.

```python
---
def automate_knowledge_graph_construction(text):
    entities, relationships =
extract_entities_relationships(text)
    populate_graph(entities, relationships)

# Sample unstructured text
```

```
sample_text = """
Type 2 Diabetes is a chronic condition that affects the way
the body processes blood sugar. It is associated with
symptoms like high glucose levels and increased thirst. Type
2 Diabetes is treated by Metformin and lifestyle changes.
Hypertension is caused by high blood pressure and is treated
by Beta Blockers.
"""

# Automate the process
automate_knowledge_graph_construction(sample_text)
```

Explanation:

- **Function `automate_knowledge_graph_construction`:** This
  function integrates entity and relationship extraction with graph
  population, automating the knowledge graph construction from
  unstructured text.
- **Sample Text:** The provided sample text includes information about
  diseases, symptoms, and treatments, serving as input for the
  automation process.

Best Practices for Automated Knowledge Graph Construction

Automating knowledge graph construction requires careful consideration to
ensure accuracy and scalability. Here are some best practices to follow:

1. Validate Extracted Data

Automated extraction can sometimes produce incorrect entities or
relationships. Implement validation checks to ensure the integrity and
accuracy of the extracted data before populating the knowledge graph.

2. Use Domain-Specific Models

For improved accuracy, especially in specialized domains like healthcare or
finance, consider using domain-specific NLP models or fine-tuning existing
models to better recognize relevant entities and relationships.

3. Handle Ambiguities and Conflicts

Automated systems may encounter ambiguities in data. Develop strategies to resolve conflicts, such as using context clues or integrating additional data sources to disambiguate entities.

4. Incremental Updates

Instead of reconstructing the entire knowledge graph with each update, implement incremental updates that add or modify only the changed parts of the graph. This approach enhances efficiency and reduces processing time.

5. Monitor and Maintain

Continuously monitor the performance of your automated pipeline. Regular maintenance, including updating models and refining extraction rules, ensures that the knowledge graph remains accurate and up-to-date.

6.3 Fine-Tuning LLMs for Graph-Based Tasks

Fine-tuning Large Language Models (LLMs) for graph-based tasks elevates their ability to understand and generate responses grounded in the structured relationships inherent in knowledge graphs. This process customizes pre-trained models to better align with specific graph-centric applications, enhancing their performance in tasks such as question answering, recommendation systems, and semantic search. In this section, we explore the significance of fine-tuning LLMs for graph-based tasks and provide a comprehensive guide to implementing this technique effectively.

The Significance of Fine-Tuning LLMs for Graph-Based Tasks

LLMs like GPT-4 possess a vast understanding of language and general knowledge. However, to excel in graph-based applications, these models benefit from fine-tuning that incorporates domain-specific data and leverages the intricate relationships within knowledge graphs. Fine-tuning enhances the model's ability to:

- **Understand Contextual Relationships:** Grasp the nuanced connections between entities in a knowledge graph.

- **Generate Accurate Responses:** Produce outputs that are not only linguistically coherent but also factually aligned with the structured data.
- **Improve Task-Specific Performance:** Excel in applications like intelligent search, personalized recommendations, and automated reasoning by leveraging graph data.

By tailoring LLMs to recognize and utilize the patterns within knowledge graphs, fine-tuning bridges the gap between unstructured language understanding and structured data manipulation.

Approaches to Fine-Tuning LLMs for Graph-Based Tasks

Fine-tuning LLMs involves adjusting the model's parameters using domain-specific data to enhance its performance on targeted tasks. Several approaches facilitate this customization:

Supervised Fine-Tuning

Supervised fine-tuning uses labeled datasets where inputs (e.g., user queries) are paired with desired outputs (e.g., accurate answers based on the knowledge graph). This method trains the model to produce responses that align closely with the structured data.

Example Workflow:

1. **Data Preparation:** Collect pairs of user queries and corresponding answers derived from the knowledge graph.
2. **Training:** Fine-tune the LLM using these pairs, adjusting its weights to minimize the difference between its outputs and the desired answers.
3. **Evaluation:** Assess the model's performance on a validation set to ensure accuracy and relevance.

Reinforcement Learning

Reinforcement learning involves training the model through feedback mechanisms, rewarding it for generating desirable responses. This approach can refine the model's ability to reason over graph data and produce contextually appropriate answers.

Example Workflow:

1. **Define Rewards:** Establish criteria for what constitutes a successful response.
2. **Interaction:** Allow the model to generate responses based on queries.
3. **Feedback:** Provide rewards based on the quality and accuracy of the responses, guiding the model to improve over time.

Few-Shot Learning

Few-shot learning leverages a small number of examples to guide the model's behavior without extensive retraining. This method is useful when limited labeled data is available.

Example Workflow:

1. **Example Selection:** Choose representative examples that illustrate the desired output based on the knowledge graph.
2. **Prompt Engineering:** Incorporate these examples into the prompts to steer the model's responses.
3. **Inference:** Use the fine-tuned model to generate answers that reflect the patterns demonstrated in the examples.

Practical Implementation: Fine-Tuning an LLM for a Healthcare FAQ Bot

To illustrate the fine-tuning process, let's walk through an example of customizing an LLM to enhance a Healthcare FAQ Bot. This bot answers user queries about diseases, symptoms, and treatments by leveraging a knowledge graph.

Step 1: Setting Up the Environment

Ensure you have the necessary libraries and access to both the LLM and your knowledge graph. For this example, we'll use the Hugging Face Transformers library and a Neo4j database.

```bash
---
```

```
pip install transformers torch neo4j pandas
```

Step 2: Preparing the Dataset

Create a dataset comprising user queries and accurate answers derived from your knowledge graph. This dataset serves as the foundation for supervised fine-tuning.

```python
---
import pandas as pd

# Sample dataset
data = {
    'query': [
        "What are the treatments for Type 2 Diabetes?",
        "What symptoms are associated with Hypertension?"
    ],
    'answer': [
        "Type 2 Diabetes is treated with Metformin and
lifestyle changes.",
        "Hypertension is associated with symptoms like high
blood pressure and headaches."
    ]
}

df = pd.DataFrame(data)
df.to_csv('healthcare_faq.csv', index=False)
```

Step 3: Loading and Preparing the Model

Utilize the Hugging Face Transformers library to load a pre-trained LLM and prepare it for fine-tuning.

```python
---
from transformers import GPT2Tokenizer, GPT2LMHeadModel,
Trainer, TrainingArguments, TextDataset,
DataCollatorForLanguageModeling

# Load tokenizer and model
tokenizer = GPT2Tokenizer.from_pretrained('gpt2')
model = GPT2LMHeadModel.from_pretrained('gpt2')

# Add special tokens if necessary
special_tokens_dict = {'additional_special_tokens':
['[QUERY]', '[ANSWER]']}
```

```
num_added_toks =
tokenizer.add_special_tokens(special_tokens_dict)
model.resize_token_embeddings(len(tokenizer))
```

Step 4: Creating the Training Dataset

Format the dataset to include special tokens that delineate queries and answers, facilitating clearer context for the model during training.

```python
---
def format_data(df):
    formatted_text = ""
    for _, row in df.iterrows():
        formatted_text += f"[QUERY] {row['query']} [ANSWER]
{row['answer']}\n"
    with open('formatted_healthcare_faq.txt', 'w') as f:
        f.write(formatted_text)

format_data(df)
```

Step 5: Preparing the Dataset for Training

Create a `TextDataset` and a `DataCollator` to handle the training data efficiently.

```python
---
def load_dataset(file_path, tokenizer, block_size=128):
    return TextDataset(
        tokenizer=tokenizer,
        file_path=file_path,
        block_size=block_size,
        overwrite_cache=True
    )

dataset = load_dataset('formatted_healthcare_faq.txt',
tokenizer)
data_collator = DataCollatorForLanguageModeling(
    tokenizer=tokenizer, mlm=False,
)
```

Step 6: Configuring Training Arguments

Define the training parameters, such as learning rate, batch size, and number of epochs.

```python
---
training_args = TrainingArguments(
    output_dir='./fine_tuned_model',
    overwrite_output_dir=True,
    num_train_epochs=3,
    per_device_train_batch_size=2,
    save_steps=500,
    save_total_limit=2,
)
```

Step 7: Initializing the Trainer and Starting Fine-Tuning

Set up the `Trainer` and commence the fine-tuning process.

```python
---
trainer = Trainer(
    model=model,
    args=training_args,
    data_collator=data_collator,
    train_dataset=dataset,
)

trainer.train()
```

Step 8: Saving the Fine-Tuned Model

After training, save the fine-tuned model for deployment.

```python
---
trainer.save_model('./fine_tuned_model')
tokenizer.save_pretrained('./fine_tuned_model')
```

Step 9: Testing the Fine-Tuned Model

Evaluate the performance of the fine-tuned model by generating responses to sample queries.

```python
---
from transformers import pipeline

# Load the fine-tuned model
fine_tuned_model =
GPT2LMHeadModel.from_pretrained('./fine_tuned_model')
```

```
fine_tuned_tokenizer =
GPT2Tokenizer.from_pretrained('./fine_tuned_model')

# Initialize the pipeline
qa_pipeline = pipeline('text-generation',
model=fine_tuned_model, tokenizer=fine_tuned_tokenizer)

# Generate a response
query = "What are the treatments for Type 2 Diabetes?"
input_text = f"[QUERY] {query} [ANSWER]"
response = qa_pipeline(input_text, max_length=100,
num_return_sequences=1)
print(response[0]['generated_text'])
```

Expected Output:

```
python
---
[QUERY] What are the treatments for Type 2 Diabetes? [ANSWER]
Type 2 Diabetes is treated with Metformin and lifestyle
changes.
```

Best Practices for Fine-Tuning LLMs for Graph-Based Tasks

To ensure effective fine-tuning of LLMs for graph-based tasks, consider the following best practices:

- **High-Quality, Domain-Specific Data:**
  Utilize datasets that accurately reflect the domain and the specific tasks your application aims to perform. High-quality data ensures that the model learns relevant patterns and relationships.
- **Balanced Dataset:**
  Ensure that your training data covers a wide range of queries and scenarios to prevent the model from becoming biased towards certain types of responses.
- **Regular Evaluation:**
  Continuously assess the model's performance using validation sets and real-world queries. This helps in identifying areas for improvement and prevents overfitting.
- **Iterative Refinement:**
  Fine-tuning is often an iterative process. Regularly update your dataset and retrain the model to incorporate new information and refine its capabilities.

- **Optimize Hyperparameters:**
  Experiment with different hyperparameters, such as learning rate and batch size, to find the optimal settings that yield the best performance for your specific tasks.
- **Leverage Transfer Learning:**
  Start with a pre-trained model that already understands general language patterns. Fine-tuning builds upon this foundation, allowing the model to adapt to specialized tasks more efficiently.

Conclusion

Fine-tuning LLMs for graph-based tasks bridges the gap between general language understanding and specialized, context-aware applications. By customizing pre-trained models with domain-specific data and leveraging the structured relationships within knowledge graphs, you enhance the model's ability to generate accurate, relevant, and contextually informed responses. The step-by-step guide provided demonstrates a practical approach to fine-tuning, ensuring that your Graph RAG systems are both intelligent and reliable.

Implementing these techniques not only improves the performance of your applications but also opens the door to more sophisticated functionalities, such as nuanced semantic search and personalized recommendations. As you continue to explore and refine fine-tuning methods, your ability to create powerful, graph-enhanced language models will significantly advance, enabling more intelligent and responsive systems.

6.4 Scaling Graph RAG for Large Datasets

As your Graph RAG (Retrieval-Augmented Generation) application grows, so does the complexity and volume of the data it handles. Scaling your system to efficiently manage large datasets is crucial for maintaining performance, ensuring reliability, and providing a seamless user experience. This section delves into the challenges of scaling Graph RAG systems and presents effective strategies and practical implementations to overcome these obstacles. By the end, you'll have a comprehensive understanding of how to scale your Graph RAG pipeline to handle extensive data seamlessly.

Understanding the Challenges of Scaling

Scaling a Graph RAG system involves addressing several key challenges:

1. **Data Volume:** As the dataset grows, storing and managing vast amounts of interconnected data becomes increasingly complex.
2. **Query Performance:** Large graphs can lead to slower query responses if not optimized properly.
3. **Resource Management:** Ensuring that computational and storage resources are efficiently utilized to handle large-scale operations.
4. **Data Consistency:** Maintaining consistency across distributed systems, especially when updates occur in real-time.
5. **Maintenance Overhead:** Increased data volume necessitates more robust maintenance strategies to prevent data degradation and ensure system integrity.

Addressing these challenges requires a combination of architectural decisions, optimized algorithms, and leveraging scalable technologies.

Strategies for Scaling Graph RAG Systems

Scaling your Graph RAG pipeline effectively involves several strategies that work in tandem to enhance performance and manage large datasets efficiently:

1. Distributed Graph Databases

Transitioning to distributed graph databases is a fundamental step in scaling. Unlike single-instance databases, distributed systems can handle larger datasets by spreading data across multiple nodes.

Key Distributed Graph Databases:

- **TigerGraph:** Designed for real-time analytics and high scalability, TigerGraph supports large-scale graphs and complex queries with low latency.

- **Dgraph:** A highly scalable, open-source graph database that offers horizontal scaling and efficient distributed query processing.
- **Amazon Neptune:** A fully managed graph database service in AWS, supporting both property graph and RDF models, and designed for high availability and scalability.

Benefits:

- **Horizontal Scalability:** Easily add more nodes to accommodate growing data without significant downtime.
- **Fault Tolerance:** Distributed systems offer redundancy, ensuring data availability even if some nodes fail.
- **Improved Performance:** Parallel processing across multiple nodes enhances query speed and overall system responsiveness.

2. Sharding and Partitioning

Sharding involves dividing the graph into smaller, more manageable segments called shards, which are distributed across different servers or clusters. Partitioning ensures that related data resides within the same shard to minimize cross-shard queries, which can be costly in terms of performance.

Implementation Steps:

1. **Identify Sharding Keys:** Choose keys based on frequently accessed entities or relationships to optimize data locality.
2. **Distribute Shards:** Allocate shards across available nodes to balance the load evenly.
3. **Optimize Queries:** Design queries to target specific shards, reducing the need for cross-shard operations.

Example:

For a social network graph, sharding could be based on user IDs, ensuring that all connections and interactions of a particular user are contained within a single shard.

3. Parallel Processing and Query Optimization

Leveraging parallel processing allows your system to handle multiple queries simultaneously, significantly improving throughput. Combining this with optimized query structures ensures that each query executes efficiently.

Techniques:

- **Parallel Query Execution:** Distribute different parts of a query across multiple nodes to execute concurrently.
- **Batch Processing:** Group similar queries and process them together to reduce overhead.
- **Query Caching:** Store the results of frequently executed queries to serve them quickly without repeated computation.

Implementation Example:

Using a distributed graph database like Dgraph, you can execute parallel queries by distributing the workload across its multiple servers, thus reducing individual query response times.

4. Efficient Data Storage and Compression

Optimizing how data is stored can significantly impact both storage costs and query performance. Techniques such as data compression and using efficient storage formats help manage large datasets more effectively.

Strategies:

- **Data Compression:** Compress graph data to reduce storage space and improve I/O performance.
- **Efficient Encoding:** Use binary formats or specialized encoding schemes to store graph structures compactly.
- **Index Optimization:** Maintain optimized indexes to facilitate quick data retrieval without excessive storage overhead.

5. Auto-Scaling Infrastructure

Implementing auto-scaling ensures that your system can dynamically adjust resources based on the current workload. This flexibility is crucial for handling varying query loads and data growth without manual intervention.

Approaches:

- **Cloud-Based Solutions:** Utilize cloud platforms like AWS, Azure, or Google Cloud, which offer auto-scaling capabilities for compute and storage resources.
- **Containerization:** Deploy graph databases within containers orchestrated by systems like Kubernetes, enabling seamless scaling based on predefined metrics.

Example:

Deploying Amazon Neptune on AWS allows you to set up auto-scaling policies that automatically adjust the number of instances based on CPU usage or memory consumption, ensuring optimal performance during peak times.

Practical Implementation: Scaling with Neo4j and Kubernetes

To illustrate the scaling process, we'll walk through an example of deploying a Neo4j graph database on Kubernetes, enabling horizontal scaling and high availability.

Step 1: Setting Up Kubernetes Cluster

Ensure you have access to a Kubernetes cluster. You can set up a local cluster using tools like Minikube or leverage cloud-based Kubernetes services such as Google Kubernetes Engine (GKE), Amazon Elastic Kubernetes Service (EKS), or Azure Kubernetes Service (AKS).

Example using Minikube:

```bash
---
# Start a local Kubernetes cluster
minikube start
```

Step 2: Deploying Neo4j on Kubernetes

Use the official Neo4j Helm chart to deploy Neo4j, which simplifies the setup process and ensures best practices are followed.

1. **Add the Neo4j Helm Repository:**

```bash
bash
---
helm repo add neo4j https://helm.neo4j.com/neo4j
helm repo update
```

2. Install Neo4j Using Helm:

```bash
bash
---
helm install my-neo4j neo4j/neo4j
```

This command deploys Neo4j with default configurations. For customized settings, create a `values.yaml` file and specify parameters such as replica count, resource limits, and storage configurations.

3. Verify Deployment:

```bash
bash
---
kubectl get pods
```

Ensure that all Neo4j pods are running successfully.

Step 3: Configuring Horizontal Pod Autoscaling

Set up Kubernetes Horizontal Pod Autoscaler (HPA) to automatically adjust the number of Neo4j replicas based on CPU utilization.

1. Define Resource Requests and Limits:

Update the `values.yaml` file to specify CPU requests and limits for Neo4j pods.

```yaml
yaml
---
resources:
  requests:
    memory: "2Gi"
    cpu: "500m"
  limits:
    memory: "4Gi"
    cpu: "1000m"
```

2. Apply the Configuration:

```bash
---
helm upgrade my-neo4j neo4j/neo4j -f values.yaml
```

3. Create the Horizontal Pod Autoscaler:

```bash
---
kubectl autoscale deployment my-neo4j-neo4j --cpu-percent=50
--min=1 --max=5
```

This configuration scales the Neo4j deployment between 1 and 5 replicas based on CPU usage, maintaining performance during high-load periods.

Step 4: Implementing Load Balancing

Use Kubernetes services to distribute incoming traffic evenly across Neo4j replicas, ensuring that no single pod becomes a bottleneck.

1. Expose Neo4j Service:

```bash
---
kubectl expose deployment my-neo4j-neo4j --type=LoadBalancer
--name=my-neo4j-service
```

2. Configure Load Balancer:

> The Kubernetes service automatically handles load balancing across available replicas. Ensure that your clients connect to the service endpoint to benefit from this distribution.

Step 5: Monitoring and Logging

Implement monitoring and logging to track the performance and health of your Neo4j deployment.

1. Install Prometheus and Grafana:

```bash
---
helm install prometheus stable/prometheus
helm install grafana stable/grafana
```

2. **Configure Neo4j Metrics Exporter:**

Use the Neo4j Exporter to expose metrics to Prometheus, enabling comprehensive monitoring of graph performance.

3. **Set Up Dashboards:**

Create Grafana dashboards to visualize key metrics such as query latency, CPU usage, memory consumption, and replication status.

Best Practices for Scaling Graph RAG Systems

Implementing effective scaling strategies ensures that your Graph RAG pipeline remains robust and performant as it handles larger datasets. Here are some best practices to consider:

- **Design for Scalability from the Start:** Architect your system with scalability in mind, choosing technologies and patterns that support growth.
- **Optimize Data Models:** Ensure that your graph schema is designed to minimize redundancy and facilitate efficient querying.
- **Leverage Caching Wisely:** Implement caching strategies to reduce database load, but balance it with data freshness to maintain accuracy.
- **Monitor Continuously:** Use monitoring tools to gain visibility into system performance, enabling proactive identification and resolution of issues.
- **Automate Deployment and Scaling:** Utilize automation tools like Helm for Kubernetes deployments and auto-scaling policies to manage resources dynamically.
- **Ensure Data Consistency:** Implement strong consistency models and transactional operations to maintain data integrity across distributed systems.
- **Plan for Disaster Recovery:** Set up backup and recovery procedures to protect against data loss and ensure business continuity.

Conclusion

Scaling Graph RAG systems to handle large datasets is a multifaceted endeavor that involves addressing data volume, query performance, resource management, and system reliability. By adopting distributed graph databases, implementing sharding and partitioning, leveraging parallel processing, optimizing data storage, and utilizing auto-scaling infrastructure, you can build a scalable and efficient Graph RAG pipeline.

The practical implementation using Neo4j and Kubernetes demonstrates how to deploy a scalable graph database in a containerized environment, ensuring high availability and performance. Adhering to best practices further solidifies your system's ability to handle growth seamlessly.

As your Graph RAG application continues to evolve, these scaling strategies will empower you to maintain optimal performance, deliver timely and accurate responses, and provide a robust foundation for advanced functionalities. Embracing these techniques ensures that your intelligent systems remain resilient, efficient, and capable of meeting the demands of expanding data landscapes.

Chapter 7: Applications and Use Cases

Graph RAG (Retrieval-Augmented Generation) systems have revolutionized how organizations harness and utilize data across various industries. By seamlessly integrating graph databases with powerful language models, these systems enable intelligent, context-aware applications that deliver enhanced insights and user experiences. This chapter explores diverse applications of Graph RAG, highlighting their impact and implementation in key sectors such as healthcare, finance, e-commerce, and beyond.

7.1 Healthcare: Intelligent Medical Queries

The healthcare industry generates and relies on vast amounts of data, encompassing patient records, medical research, treatment protocols, and more. Navigating this complex landscape to extract meaningful insights can be daunting. Intelligent Medical Queries, powered by Graph RAG (Retrieval-Augmented Generation) systems, offer a transformative solution. By integrating graph databases with advanced language models, these systems enable healthcare professionals to access precise, contextually relevant information swiftly and accurately. This section explores the significance, applications, and implementation of Intelligent Medical Queries in healthcare.

The Role of Intelligent Medical Queries in Healthcare

Healthcare professionals often face the challenge of sifting through extensive data to find relevant information. Whether it's diagnosing a patient, planning a treatment, or conducting research, the ability to retrieve accurate and comprehensive data efficiently is crucial. Intelligent Medical Queries address this need by leveraging the interconnected nature of medical data, enabling seamless access to relevant information.

Enhancing Diagnostic Processes

Accurate diagnosis is the cornerstone of effective treatment. Intelligent Medical Queries assist clinicians by providing quick access to a wealth of medical knowledge, including symptoms, diseases, treatments, and patient histories. By understanding the relationships between various medical entities, these systems can offer differential diagnoses and suggest potential conditions based on the input symptoms.

For instance, when a doctor inputs specific symptoms into the system, the Intelligent Medical Query can retrieve related diseases, their prevalence, associated symptoms, and recommended treatments. This not only speeds up the diagnostic process but also enhances its accuracy by ensuring that no potential condition is overlooked.

Personalizing Treatment Plans

Every patient is unique, with distinct medical histories, genetic profiles, and lifestyle factors. Intelligent Medical Queries enable the creation of personalized treatment plans by analyzing a patient's specific data within the broader context of medical knowledge. By integrating patient records with the latest research and treatment protocols, these systems can suggest tailored treatment options that align with the patient's individual needs.

For example, considering a patient's medical history, current medications, and genetic markers, the system can recommend treatments that are more likely to be effective and have fewer side effects. This personalized approach not only improves patient outcomes but also enhances overall healthcare efficiency.

Facilitating Medical Research and Knowledge Management

Medical research is an ever-evolving field, with new studies and discoveries emerging regularly. Keeping abreast of the latest developments is essential for healthcare professionals. Intelligent Medical Queries streamline this process by automating the retrieval and synthesis of relevant research findings.

Researchers can use these systems to identify gaps in existing knowledge, explore new treatment avenues, and stay updated with the latest advancements. By integrating diverse data sources, including clinical trials, medical journals, and case studies, Intelligent Medical Queries provide a comprehensive view of the current state of medical research, fostering informed decision-making and innovation.

Implementing Intelligent Medical Queries with Graph RAG Systems

Integrating Intelligent Medical Queries into healthcare systems involves several key steps, each leveraging the strengths of graph databases and language models to deliver precise and context-aware information.

1. Building a Comprehensive Knowledge Graph

At the heart of Intelligent Medical Queries lies a well-structured knowledge graph. This graph maps out the relationships between various medical entities, such as diseases, symptoms, treatments, medications, and patient profiles. By representing data in a graph format, the system can efficiently traverse and query the intricate web of medical information.

Key Components:

- **Entities:** Represented as nodes, these include diseases, symptoms, treatments, medications, healthcare providers, and patient records.
- **Relationships:** Represented as edges, these illustrate how entities interact, such as "causes," "treated by," "associated with," and "prescribed for."

2. Integrating Graph Databases with LLMs

Graph databases like Neo4j store and manage the knowledge graph, while Large Language Models (LLMs) like GPT-4 handle the natural language processing aspect. By integrating these technologies, Intelligent Medical Queries can interpret user inputs, traverse the knowledge graph, and generate coherent, contextually relevant responses.

Integration Process:

- **Data Retrieval:** The LLM processes the user query to identify key entities and intents. It then translates these into graph queries to retrieve relevant data from the graph database.
- **Response Generation:** The retrieved data is fed back into the LLM, which formulates a natural language response that is both informative and contextually appropriate.

3. Ensuring Data Accuracy and Privacy

In healthcare, data accuracy and patient privacy are paramount. Implementing robust data validation mechanisms ensures that the information retrieved and generated by Intelligent Medical Queries is accurate and reliable. Additionally, adhering to data privacy regulations, such as HIPAA, is essential to protect sensitive patient information.

Best Practices:

- **Data Validation:** Regularly verify the accuracy of the data within the knowledge graph through automated checks and manual reviews.
- **Access Controls:** Implement strict access controls and authentication measures to ensure that only authorized personnel can access sensitive data.
- **Anonymization:** Anonymize patient data where necessary to protect individual identities and comply with privacy regulations.

Challenges and Solutions in Implementing Intelligent Medical Queries

While Intelligent Medical Queries offer significant advantages, their implementation comes with challenges that must be addressed to ensure effectiveness and reliability.

Data Integration and Standardization

Integrating data from diverse sources—such as electronic health records (EHRs), research databases, and clinical trials—requires standardization to maintain consistency within the knowledge graph.

Solution:

- **Use of Standards:** Adopt standardized medical terminologies and ontologies, such as SNOMED CT and ICD-10, to ensure uniformity across different data sources.
- **Automated ETL Processes:** Implement automated Extract, Transform, Load (ETL) processes to streamline data integration and reduce manual intervention.

Scalability and Performance

As the volume of medical data grows, ensuring that the system remains responsive and efficient becomes increasingly challenging.

Solution:

- **Distributed Graph Databases:** Utilize distributed graph databases that can handle large-scale data across multiple nodes, enhancing performance and scalability.
- **Efficient Query Optimization:** Implement advanced query optimization techniques to ensure that data retrieval remains swift, even as the graph expands.

Maintaining Data Privacy and Security

Protecting patient data is critical, and any breach can have severe consequences.

Solution:

- **Encryption:** Encrypt data both at rest and in transit to safeguard against unauthorized access.
- **Regular Audits:** Conduct regular security audits and vulnerability assessments to identify and mitigate potential threats.
- **Compliance:** Ensure that the system complies with all relevant data protection regulations and standards.

Best Practices for Implementing Intelligent Medical Queries

To maximize the effectiveness and reliability of Intelligent Medical Queries in healthcare, consider the following best practices:

Comprehensive Data Modeling

Develop a detailed and comprehensive data model that accurately represents the relationships and hierarchies within the medical domain. A well-designed knowledge graph facilitates efficient data retrieval and accurate response generation.

Continuous Learning and Updating

Healthcare knowledge is constantly evolving. Implement mechanisms for continuous learning and regular updates to the knowledge graph to incorporate the latest medical research and clinical guidelines.

User-Centric Design

Design the system with the end-user in mind. Ensure that the interface is intuitive and that the responses generated are clear, concise, and actionable, catering to the needs of healthcare professionals.

Robust Testing and Validation

Regularly test the system with a wide range of queries to ensure accuracy and reliability. Use both automated testing and manual reviews to validate the responses generated by Intelligent Medical Queries.

Collaboration with Medical Experts

Work closely with healthcare professionals during the development and implementation phases. Their insights are invaluable in ensuring that the system meets clinical needs and adheres to medical standards.

Conclusion

Intelligent Medical Queries, powered by Graph RAG systems, represent a significant advancement in how healthcare professionals access and utilize medical data. By integrating graph databases with sophisticated language models, these systems provide accurate, contextually relevant information that enhances diagnostic accuracy, personalizes treatment plans, and supports ongoing medical research. While implementing such systems presents challenges, adopting best practices and leveraging the right technologies can overcome these obstacles, ensuring that Intelligent Medical Queries deliver substantial benefits to the healthcare industry.

As the healthcare landscape continues to evolve, the role of Intelligent Medical Queries will become increasingly vital, driving improvements in patient care, operational efficiency, and medical innovation. Embracing these advanced technologies equips healthcare providers with the tools necessary to navigate the complexities of modern medicine, ultimately leading to better health outcomes and a more responsive healthcare system.

7.2 Finance: Risk Assessment and Fraud Detection

In the fast-paced world of finance, safeguarding assets and ensuring the integrity of transactions are paramount. Risk assessment and fraud detection play critical roles in maintaining the stability and trustworthiness of financial institutions. Graph RAG (Retrieval-Augmented Generation) systems offer advanced solutions by harnessing the power of graph databases and sophisticated language models to analyze complex relationships and patterns within financial data. This section delves into how Graph RAG enhances risk assessment and fraud detection, explores its significance, and provides a practical guide to implementing these systems effectively.

The Importance of Risk Assessment and Fraud Detection in Finance

Financial institutions operate in environments where risks and fraudulent activities can have significant repercussions. Effective risk assessment enables organizations to identify, evaluate, and mitigate potential threats, ensuring operational continuity and regulatory compliance. Fraud detection, on the other hand, protects both the institution and its customers from illicit activities that can lead to substantial financial losses and reputational damage.

Traditional approaches to risk assessment and fraud detection often rely on rule-based systems and statistical models. While these methods can be effective to an extent, they may fall short in identifying intricate patterns and adapting to evolving fraudulent schemes. This is where Graph RAG systems come into play, offering a more dynamic and intelligent approach by leveraging the interconnected nature of financial data.

Enhancing Risk Assessment with Graph RAG Systems

Risk assessment in finance involves analyzing various factors, including creditworthiness, market volatility, and operational risks. Graph RAG systems enhance this process by integrating diverse data sources into a unified knowledge graph, enabling a holistic view of potential risks.

Holistic Data Integration:
Financial data is inherently interconnected, with relationships spanning across transactions, accounts, market indicators, and external factors like economic trends. Graph databases excel in representing these complex relationships, allowing risk analysts to traverse and explore connections that might not be evident through traditional data structures.

Predictive Insights:
By combining graph databases with Large Language Models (LLMs), Graph RAG systems can generate predictive insights based on historical data and emerging patterns. For instance, the system can identify correlations between seemingly unrelated factors, such as specific transaction behaviors and market downturns, providing early warnings for potential risks.

Dynamic Risk Modeling:
Financial environments are constantly evolving, with new risks emerging as markets and technologies advance. Graph RAG systems offer the flexibility to update and expand the knowledge graph in real-time, ensuring that risk models remain current and responsive to changes.

Revolutionizing Fraud Detection with Graph RAG Systems

Fraud detection is a critical function in finance, aiming to identify and prevent unauthorized or deceptive activities. Graph RAG systems bring a new level of sophistication to fraud detection by uncovering hidden patterns and relationships within transactional data.

Uncovering Hidden Connections:
Fraudulent activities often involve networks of accounts and transactions designed to conceal illicit actions. Graph databases can map these intricate networks, revealing connections between seemingly unrelated entities. This capability allows fraud detection systems to identify suspicious clusters and anomalous behaviors that traditional methods might overlook.

Real-Time Anomaly Detection:
Graph RAG systems can process and analyze transactions in real-time, enabling immediate detection of anomalies. By continuously updating the

knowledge graph with new data, the system can swiftly identify deviations from established patterns, triggering alerts for further investigation.

Adaptive Learning:
Fraudsters continually adapt their strategies to evade detection. Graph RAG systems, equipped with LLMs, can learn from new fraud patterns and adjust their detection algorithms accordingly. This adaptive learning ensures that fraud detection remains robust against evolving threats.

Practical Implementation: Building a Fraud Detection System with Graph RAG

To illustrate how Graph RAG systems can be implemented for fraud detection, let's walk through a step-by-step example using Neo4j as the graph database and Python for data processing and integration with an LLM.

Step 1: Setting Up the Environment

Begin by installing the necessary tools and libraries. You'll need Neo4j for managing the graph database and Python libraries for data manipulation and integration.

```bash
---
# Install Neo4j
# Download and install Neo4j from https://neo4j.com/download/

# Install Python libraries
pip install neo4j pandas scikit-learn openai
```

Step 2: Initializing Neo4j and Creating the Knowledge Graph

Start by defining the structure of your knowledge graph, focusing on entities and their relationships relevant to fraud detection, such as accounts, transactions, devices, and locations.

```python
---
from neo4j import GraphDatabase

# Neo4j connection details
NEO4J_URI = "bolt://localhost:7687"
```

```python
NEO4J_USER = "neo4j"
NEO4J_PASSWORD = "your_password"

# Initialize the Neo4j driver
driver = GraphDatabase.driver(NEO4J_URI, auth=(NEO4J_USER,
NEO4J_PASSWORD))

def create_entities_and_relationships():
    with driver.session() as session:
        # Create sample accounts
        session.run("MERGE (a:Account {id: 'A1'})")
        session.run("MERGE (a:Account {id: 'A2'})")
        session.run("MERGE (a:Account {id: 'A3'})")

        # Create sample transactions
        session.run("""
            MERGE (t1:Transaction {id: 'T1', amount: 1000,
timestamp: '2024-01-01'})
            MERGE (t2:Transaction {id: 'T2', amount: 2000,
timestamp: '2024-01-02'})
            MERGE (t3:Transaction {id: 'T3', amount: 1500,
timestamp: '2024-01-03'})
        """)

        # Create relationships between accounts and
transactions
        session.run("""
            MATCH (a:Account {id: 'A1'}), (t:Transaction {id:
'T1'})
            MERGE (a)-[:MADE]->(t)
        """)
        session.run("""
            MATCH (a:Account {id: 'A2'}), (t:Transaction {id:
'T2'})
            MERGE (a)-[:MADE]->(t)
        """)
        session.run("""
            MATCH (a:Account {id: 'A3'}), (t:Transaction {id:
'T3'})
            MERGE (a)-[:MADE]->(t)
        """)

        # Create devices and locations
        session.run("""
            MERGE (d1:Device {id: 'D1', type: 'Mobile'})
            MERGE (d2:Device {id: 'D2', type: 'Desktop'})
            MERGE (l1:Location {id: 'L1', city: 'New York'})
            MERGE (l2:Location {id: 'L2', city: 'Los
Angeles'})
        """)
```

```
        # Create relationships between transactions and
devices/locations
        session.run("""
            MATCH (t:Transaction {id: 'T1'}), (d:Device {id:
'D1'}), (l:Location {id: 'L1'})
            MERGE (t)-[:INITIATED_FROM]->(d)
            MERGE (t)-[:LOCATED_AT]->(l)
        """)
        session.run("""
            MATCH (t:Transaction {id: 'T2'}), (d:Device {id:
'D2'}), (l:Location {id: 'L2'})
            MERGE (t)-[:INITIATED_FROM]->(d)
            MERGE (t)-[:LOCATED_AT]->(l)
        """)
        session.run("""
            MATCH (t:Transaction {id: 'T3'}), (d:Device {id:
'D1'}), (l:Location {id: 'L1'})
            MERGE (t)-[:INITIATED_FROM]->(d)
            MERGE (t)-[:LOCATED_AT]->(l)
        """)

create_entities_and_relationships()

# Close the driver
driver.close()
```

Explanation:

This script initializes a simple knowledge graph with accounts, transactions, devices, and locations, establishing relationships that are crucial for detecting fraudulent activities.

Step 3: Integrating Transaction Data and Identifying Anomalies

Next, incorporate transaction data and implement anomaly detection using machine learning techniques. Suspicious patterns can then be flagged for further investigation.

```python
python
---
import pandas as pd
from sklearn.ensemble import IsolationForest

# Sample transaction data
data = {
    'transaction_id': ['T1', 'T2', 'T3', 'T4', 'T5'],
    'account_id': ['A1', 'A2', 'A3', 'A1', 'A2'],
    'amount': [1000, 2000, 1500, 5000, 3000],
    'device_id': ['D1', 'D2', 'D1', 'D3', 'D2'],
```

```
    'location_id': ['L1', 'L2', 'L1', 'L3', 'L2'],
    'timestamp': ['2024-01-01', '2024-01-02', '2024-01-03',
'2024-01-04', '2024-01-05']
}

df = pd.DataFrame(data)

# Feature Engineering
df['amount_log'] = df['amount'].apply(lambda x: np.log(x +
1))
df['day_of_week'] =
pd.to_datetime(df['timestamp']).dt.dayofweek

# Isolation Forest for Anomaly Detection
model = IsolationForest(contamination=0.2, random_state=42)
df['anomaly_score'] = model.fit_predict(df[['amount_log',
'day_of_week']])

# Flag anomalies
df['is_fraud'] = df['anomaly_score'].apply(lambda x: 'Yes' if
x == -1 else 'No')
print(df)
```

Explanation:

This script uses the Isolation Forest algorithm to detect anomalies in transaction amounts and their occurrence days. Transactions flagged as anomalies are potential candidates for fraud.

Step 4: Updating the Knowledge Graph with Anomaly Information

Incorporate the anomaly information back into the knowledge graph to enrich the data and enable more sophisticated fraud detection queries.

```python
---
from neo4j import GraphDatabase

# Reinitialize the Neo4j driver
driver = GraphDatabase.driver(NEO4J_URI, auth=(NEO4J_USER,
NEO4J_PASSWORD))

def update_fraud_status(df):
    with driver.session() as session:
        for _, row in df.iterrows():
            fraud_status = row['is_fraud']
            transaction_id = row['transaction_id']
            session.run("""
                MATCH (t:Transaction {id: $tid})
                SET t.fraud = $fraud
```

```
            """, tid=transaction_id, fraud=fraud_status)

update_fraud_status(df)

# Close the driver
driver.close()
```

Explanation:

This function updates each transaction node in Neo4j with a `fraud` property indicating whether it has been flagged as fraudulent.

Step 5: Leveraging Graph RAG for Enhanced Fraud Detection

Combine the structured data in Neo4j with a language model to generate insightful reports and predictions based on the relationships within the knowledge graph.

```python
---
import openai

# Set up OpenAI API key
openai.api_key = 'your_openai_api_key'

def generate_fraud_report(transaction_id):
    with driver.session() as session:
        result = session.run("""
            MATCH (a:Account)-[:MADE]->(t:Transaction {id:
$tid})-[:INITIATED_FROM]->(d:Device),
                  (t)-[:LOCATED_AT]->(l:Location)
            RETURN a.id AS account, t.amount AS amount,
d.type AS device, l.city AS city, t.fraud AS fraud
        """, tid=transaction_id)
        record = result.single()
        if record:
            account = record['account']
            amount = record['amount']
            device = record['device']
            city = record['city']
            fraud = record['fraud']
            context = f"Account ID: {account}\nAmount:
{amount}\nDevice Type: {device}\nLocation:
{city}\nFraudulent: {fraud}"

            prompt = f"Analyze the following transaction
details and provide insights:\n{context}\nInsights:"

            response = openai.Completion.create(
                engine="text-davinci-004",
```

```
                prompt=prompt,
                max_tokens=150
        )

        return response.choices[0].text.strip()
    else:
        return "Transaction not found."

# Example usage
report = generate_fraud_report('T4')
print(report)
```

Explanation:
This function retrieves transaction details from Neo4j and uses OpenAI's GPT-4 to generate an insightful analysis, helping analysts understand the context and potential reasons behind a flagged transaction.

Best Practices for Implementing Graph RAG in Finance

To maximize the effectiveness of Graph RAG systems in risk assessment and fraud detection, adhere to the following best practices:

Comprehensive Data Integration:
Ensure that all relevant data sources are integrated into the knowledge graph. This includes transactional data, customer profiles, device information, and external data such as market indicators. Comprehensive integration provides a holistic view, enabling more accurate risk assessments and fraud detection.

Continuous Learning and Model Updating:
Financial fraud tactics evolve rapidly. Implement mechanisms for continuous learning, allowing the system to adapt to new patterns and strategies. Regularly update both the knowledge graph and the language models to incorporate the latest data and insights.

Robust Validation and Testing:
Regularly validate the system's outputs to ensure accuracy and reliability. Use historical data to test the system's ability to detect known fraudulent activities and assess its performance in risk prediction scenarios.

Data Privacy and Security:
Protect sensitive financial data by implementing strong security measures. Ensure compliance with regulations such as GDPR and PCI DSS, and

employ encryption, access controls, and regular security audits to safeguard data integrity and confidentiality.

Scalability and Performance Optimization:
As the volume of financial data grows, optimize the system for scalability. Utilize distributed graph databases, efficient query optimization techniques, and caching mechanisms to maintain high performance and responsiveness.

Collaboration with Financial Experts:
Work closely with financial analysts and domain experts to fine-tune the system. Their insights are invaluable in refining detection algorithms, interpreting results, and ensuring that the system aligns with real-world financial practices and regulations.

Conclusion

Graph RAG systems offer a transformative approach to risk assessment and fraud detection in the finance industry. By integrating the relational power of graph databases with the contextual intelligence of language models, these systems enable financial institutions to uncover hidden patterns, predict potential risks, and detect fraudulent activities with unprecedented accuracy and efficiency.

The practical implementation guide provided illustrates how to build a fraud detection system that leverages Neo4j for managing complex relationships and Python for data processing and integration with an LLM. By following these steps and adhering to best practices, financial organizations can enhance their ability to safeguard assets, comply with regulatory requirements, and maintain the trust of their customers.

7.3 E-Commerce: Personalization and Recommendations

In the competitive landscape of e-commerce, delivering personalized experiences and accurate recommendations can significantly influence customer satisfaction and sales. Graph RAG (Retrieval-Augmented Generation) systems empower e-commerce platforms to understand customer behaviors, preferences, and interactions at a granular level, driving more effective personalization strategies. This section explores the role of

Graph RAG in enhancing personalization and recommendations, delves into its benefits, and provides a practical guide to implementing these capabilities in an e-commerce setting.

The Importance of Personalization and Recommendations in E-Commerce

Personalization and recommendations are pivotal in creating engaging and satisfying shopping experiences. By tailoring interactions and suggestions to individual customers, e-commerce platforms can increase conversion rates, foster customer loyalty, and boost overall sales. Traditional recommendation systems often rely on collaborative filtering or content-based approaches, which, while effective, may fall short in capturing the intricate relationships between products, customers, and their behaviors. Graph RAG systems address these limitations by leveraging the interconnected nature of data, enabling more nuanced and context-aware recommendations.

Enhancing Personalization with Graph RAG Systems

Graph RAG systems integrate graph databases with powerful language models to provide a comprehensive understanding of customer interactions and product relationships. This integration facilitates the creation of personalized shopping experiences by analyzing complex data patterns and generating relevant recommendations.

Understanding Customer Behaviors: Graph databases excel at representing complex relationships between entities. In an e-commerce context, entities can include customers, products, categories, reviews, and interactions such as purchases, views, and ratings. By mapping these relationships, Graph RAG systems can uncover deep insights into customer preferences and behaviors.

Context-Aware Recommendations: Unlike traditional systems that may only consider past purchases or ratings, Graph RAG systems analyze the broader context, including browsing history, product similarities, seasonal trends, and even social influences. This comprehensive analysis ensures that recommendations are not only relevant but also timely and aligned with the customer's current needs.

Dynamic Personalization: E-commerce environments are dynamic, with constantly changing inventory, trends, and customer preferences. Graph RAG systems enable real-time personalization by continuously updating the knowledge graph with new data, ensuring that recommendations evolve alongside the market and individual customer journeys.

Practical Implementation: Building a Personalized Recommendation System with Graph RAG

To demonstrate how Graph RAG can enhance personalization and recommendations in e-commerce, we'll walk through a practical implementation using Neo4j as the graph database and Python for data processing and integration with a language model like GPT-4.

Step 1: Setting Up the Environment

Begin by installing the necessary tools and libraries. You'll need Neo4j for managing the graph database and Python libraries for data manipulation and integration with the language model.

```bash
---
# Install Neo4j
# Download and install Neo4j from https://neo4j.com/download/

# Install Python libraries
pip install neo4j pandas openai
```

Step 2: Initializing Neo4j and Creating the Knowledge Graph

Start by defining the structure of your knowledge graph, focusing on entities and their relationships relevant to e-commerce, such as customers, products, categories, and interactions.

```python
---
from neo4j import GraphDatabase

# Neo4j connection details
```

```python
NEO4J_URI = "bolt://localhost:7687"
NEO4J_USER = "neo4j"
NEO4J_PASSWORD = "your_password"

# Initialize the Neo4j driver
driver = GraphDatabase.driver(NEO4J_URI, auth=(NEO4J_USER,
NEO4J_PASSWORD))

def create_entities_and_relationships():
    with driver.session() as session:
        # Create sample customers
        session.run("MERGE (c1:Customer {id: 'C1', name:
'Alice'})")
        session.run("MERGE (c2:Customer {id: 'C2', name:
'Bob'})")
        session.run("MERGE (c3:Customer {id: 'C3', name:
'Charlie'})")

        # Create sample products
        session.run("MERGE (p1:Product {id: 'P1', name:
'Smartphone'})")
        session.run("MERGE (p2:Product {id: 'P2', name:
'Laptop'})")
        session.run("MERGE (p3:Product {id: 'P3', name:
'Headphones'})")

        # Create categories
        session.run("MERGE (cat1:Category {id: 'Cat1', name:
'Electronics'})")
        session.run("MERGE (cat2:Category {id: 'Cat2', name:
'Accessories'})")

        # Create relationships between products and
categories
        session.run("""
            MATCH (p:Product {id: 'P1'}), (c:Category {id:
'Cat1'})
            MERGE (p)-[:BELONGS_TO]->(c)
        """)
        session.run("""
            MATCH (p:Product {id: 'P2'}), (c:Category {id:
'Cat1'})
            MERGE (p)-[:BELONGS_TO]->(c)
        """)
        session.run("""
            MATCH (p:Product {id: 'P3'}), (c:Category {id:
'Cat2'})
            MERGE (p)-[:BELONGS_TO]->(c)
        """)

        # Create customer interactions
```

```
        session.run("""
            MATCH (c:Customer {id: 'C1'}), (p:Product {id:
'P1'})
            MERGE (c)-[:VIEWED]->(p)
        """)
        session.run("""
            MATCH (c:Customer {id: 'C1'}), (p:Product {id:
'P3'})
            MERGE (c)-[:PURCHASED]->(p)
        """)
        session.run("""
            MATCH (c:Customer {id: 'C2'}), (p:Product {id:
'P2'})
            MERGE (c)-[:VIEWED]->(p)
        """)
        session.run("""
            MATCH (c:Customer {id: 'C3'}), (p:Product {id:
'P3'})
            MERGE (c)-[:VIEWED]->(p)
            MERGE (c)-[:PURCHASED]->(p)
        """)

        # Create product similarities
        session.run("""
            MATCH (p1:Product {id: 'P1'}), (p2:Product {id:
'P2'})
            MERGE (p1)-[:SIMILAR_TO]->(p2)
            MERGE (p2)-[:SIMILAR_TO]->(p1)
        """)
        session.run("""
            MATCH (p1:Product {id: 'P1'}), (p3:Product {id:
'P3'})
            MERGE (p1)-[:SIMILAR_TO]->(p3)
            MERGE (p3)-[:SIMILAR_TO]->(p1)
        """)
        session.run("""
            MATCH (p2:Product {id: 'P2'}), (p3:Product {id:
'P3'})
            MERGE (p2)-[:SIMILAR_TO]->(p3)
            MERGE (p3)-[:SIMILAR_TO]->(p2)
        """)

create_entities_and_relationships()

# Close the driver
driver.close()
```

Explanation:
This script initializes a simple knowledge graph with customers, products, categories, and their interactions. Relationships such as VIEWED, PURCHASED,

BELONGS_TO, and SIMILAR_TO are established to represent the interactions and similarities essential for personalized recommendations.

Step 3: Extracting and Preparing Data for Recommendations

Retrieve data from Neo4j to analyze customer behaviors and product relationships, laying the groundwork for generating personalized recommendations.

```python
---
import pandas as pd
from neo4j import GraphDatabase

# Reinitialize the Neo4j driver
driver = GraphDatabase.driver(NEO4J_URI, auth=(NEO4J_USER,
NEO4J_PASSWORD))

def get_customer_views():
    query = """
    MATCH (c:Customer)-[:VIEWED]->(p:Product)
    RETURN c.id AS customer_id, p.id AS product_id
    """
    with driver.session() as session:
        result = session.run(query)
        data = pd.DataFrame([record.data() for record in
result])
    return data

def get_customer_purchases():
    query = """
    MATCH (c:Customer)-[:PURCHASED]->(p:Product)
    RETURN c.id AS customer_id, p.id AS product_id
    """
    with driver.session() as. session:
        result = session.run(query)
        data = pd.DataFrame([record.data() for record in
result])
    return data

def get_product_similarities():
    query = """
    MATCH (p1:Product)-[:SIMILAR_TO]->(p2:Product)
    RETURN p1.id AS product_id, p2.id AS similar_product_id
    """
    with driver.session() as session:
        result = session.run(query)
        data = pd.DataFrame([record.data() for record in
result])
```

```
    return data

views_df = get_customer_views()
purchases_df = get_customer_purchases()
similarities_df = get_product_similarities()

# Close the driver
driver.close()

print("Customer Views:")
print(views_df)
print("\nCustomer Purchases:")
print(purchases_df)
print("\nProduct Similarities:")
print(similarities_df)
```

Explanation:

This script retrieves data on customer views, purchases, and product similarities from Neo4j, storing them in pandas DataFrames for further analysis. Understanding these interactions is crucial for generating accurate and personalized recommendations.

Step 4: Building the Recommendation Engine

Utilize the extracted data to create a recommendation engine that suggests products based on customer behavior and product similarities.

```python
---
import numpy as np
from sklearn.metrics.pairwise import cosine_similarity

# Create a user-item interaction matrix
interaction_matrix = purchases_df.groupby(['customer_id',
'product_id']).size().unstack(fill_value=0)

# Normalize the interaction matrix
interaction_matrix_norm = interaction_matrix.apply(lambda x:
(x - np.mean(x)) / (np.std(x) + 1e-9), axis=1)

# Compute cosine similarity between users
user_similarity = cosine_similarity(interaction_matrix_norm)
user_similarity_df = pd.DataFrame(user_similarity,
index=interaction_matrix.index,
columns=interaction_matrix.index)

def recommend_products(customer_id, top_n=2):
    if customer_id not in user_similarity_df.index:
```

```
        return []

    # Get similarity scores for the customer
    similarity_scores = user_similarity_df[customer_id]

    # Get top similar customers
    similar_customers =
similarity_scores.sort_values(ascending=False).iloc[1:top_n+1
].index

    # Get products purchased by similar customers
    recommended_products =
purchases_df[purchases_df['customer_id'].isin(similar_custome
rs)]['product_id'].unique()

    # Exclude products already purchased by the customer
    already_purchased =
purchases_df[purchases_df['customer_id'] ==
customer_id]['product_id'].unique()
    recommendations = [prod for prod in recommended_products
if prod not in already_purchased]

    return recommendations[:top_n]

# Example usage
customer = 'C1'
recommended = recommend_products(customer, top_n=2)
print(f"Recommended products for Customer {customer}:
{recommended}")
```

Explanation:
This script builds a simple collaborative filtering recommendation engine based on user similarity. It identifies similar customers and recommends products they have purchased that the target customer hasn't yet bought. While this approach is foundational, integrating graph-based insights can further enhance recommendation accuracy.

Step 5: Integrating with a Language Model for Enhanced Recommendations

Enhance the recommendation engine by integrating a language model like GPT-4 to provide contextual and descriptive recommendations based on the graph data.

```python
---
import openai
```

```python
# Set up OpenAI API key
openai.api_key = 'your_openai_api_key'

def generate_recommendation_description(customer_id,
recommended_products):
    if not recommended_products:
        return "No recommendations available at this time."

    descriptions = []
    with driver.session() as session:
        for product_id in recommended_products:
            query = """
            MATCH (p:Product {id: $pid})-[:BELONGS_TO]-
>(c:Category)
            RETURN p.name AS product_name, c.name AS category
            """
            result = session.run(query, pid=product_id)
            record = result.single()
            if record:
                product_name = record['product_name']
                category = record['category']
                descriptions.append(f"{product_name} in
{category}")

    context = ", ".join(descriptions)
    prompt = f"Provide a personalized recommendation based on
the following products: {context}. Highlight why these
products are suitable for the customer."

    response = openai.Completion.create(
        engine="text-davinci-004",
        prompt=prompt,
        max_tokens=150
    )

    return response.choices[0].text.strip()

# Reinitialize the Neo4j driver for the new query
driver = GraphDatabase.driver(NEO4J_URI, auth=(NEO4J_USER,
NEO4J_PASSWORD))

# Example usage
description = generate_recommendation_description(customer,
recommended)
print(description)

# Close the driver
driver.close()
```

Explanation:
This script fetches detailed information about the recommended products from Neo4j and uses OpenAI's GPT-4 to generate a personalized and descriptive recommendation. The language model enhances the user experience by providing contextually rich and engaging recommendations.

Best Practices for Implementing Graph RAG in E-Commerce

To maximize the effectiveness of Graph RAG systems in e-commerce personalization and recommendations, consider the following best practices:

Comprehensive Data Integration: Ensure that all relevant data sources are integrated into the knowledge graph. This includes customer interactions, product information, reviews, and external data such as market trends. Comprehensive integration provides a holistic view, enabling more accurate and relevant recommendations.

Real-Time Data Updates: E-commerce environments are dynamic, with constantly changing inventories, customer behaviors, and market conditions. Implement real-time data ingestion and update mechanisms to keep the knowledge graph current, ensuring that recommendations reflect the latest information.

Personalization Depth: Go beyond basic purchase history by incorporating diverse data points such as browsing behavior, wish lists, product ratings, and social interactions. The richer the data, the more nuanced and effective the personalization can be.

Scalability and Performance Optimization: As your customer base and product catalog grow, ensure that your Graph RAG system scales accordingly. Utilize distributed graph databases, optimize query performance, and implement caching strategies to maintain responsiveness.

User Privacy and Data Security: Handle customer data with utmost care, adhering to privacy regulations and implementing robust security measures. Ensure that data used for personalization is anonymized where necessary and that access controls are in place to protect sensitive information.

Continuous Evaluation and Improvement: Regularly assess the performance of your recommendation system using metrics such as click-through rates, conversion rates, and customer satisfaction scores. Use these insights to refine your algorithms and update the knowledge graph, ensuring continuous improvement.

Collaborate with Stakeholders: Work closely with marketing teams, data scientists, and customer service representatives to understand the nuances of customer needs and preferences. Their insights can guide the development and optimization of the recommendation system.

Conclusion

Graph RAG systems offer a sophisticated approach to personalization and recommendations in the e-commerce sector. By integrating graph databases with advanced language models, these systems provide a deep understanding of customer behaviors and product relationships, enabling highly personalized and contextually relevant recommendations. The practical implementation guide demonstrates how to build a personalized recommendation engine using Neo4j and Python, showcasing the seamless integration of structured graph data with intelligent language models.

Adhering to best practices ensures that your Graph RAG system remains effective, scalable, and secure, delivering exceptional user experiences and driving business growth. As e-commerce continues to evolve, leveraging Graph RAG technologies will be instrumental in staying ahead of the competition, fostering customer loyalty, and maximizing sales through intelligent, personalized interactions.

7.4 Other Industry Applications

Graph RAG (Retrieval-Augmented Generation) systems extend their transformative capabilities beyond the realms of healthcare, finance, and e-commerce, finding impactful applications across a multitude of other industries. By harnessing the power of graph databases and advanced language models, these systems enable organizations to navigate complex data landscapes, uncover hidden insights, and drive innovation. This section explores diverse applications of Graph RAG in sectors such as manufacturing, telecommunications, education, energy, and human resources, illustrating how these technologies are reshaping industries by enhancing efficiency, personalization, and decision-making.

Manufacturing: Supply Chain Optimization

In the manufacturing sector, managing intricate supply chains is essential for operational efficiency and competitiveness. Graph RAG systems play a pivotal role in optimizing supply chains by mapping out the complex relationships between suppliers, manufacturers, distributors, and retailers.

Enhancing Visibility and Traceability

Supply chains are composed of numerous entities and interactions that can be challenging to monitor and manage. Graph databases excel at representing these interconnected components, providing a comprehensive view of the entire supply chain. By visualizing relationships and dependencies, manufacturers can identify bottlenecks, monitor supplier performance, and ensure the traceability of products from raw materials to end consumers.

Predictive Maintenance and Inventory Management

Graph RAG systems facilitate predictive maintenance by analyzing the relationships between machinery, components, and operational data. By identifying patterns and correlations, these systems can predict equipment failures before they occur, reducing downtime and maintenance costs. Additionally, optimized inventory management is achieved by analyzing demand patterns, supplier reliability, and lead times, ensuring that inventory levels are maintained efficiently without overstocking or stockouts.

Practical Implementation: Optimizing Supply Chains with Neo4j and Python

To demonstrate how Graph RAG can optimize supply chains, let's walk through a practical example using Neo4j and Python. This implementation will map suppliers, manufacturers, products, and distributors, enabling the identification of optimal supply routes and predictive maintenance insights.

Step 1: Setting Up the Environment

Ensure you have Neo4j installed and the necessary Python libraries.

```bash
bash
---
# Install Neo4j
# Download and install Neo4j from https://neo4j.com/download/

# Install Python libraries
pip install neo4j pandas
```

Step 2: Initializing Neo4j and Creating the Knowledge Graph

Define the entities and relationships relevant to the supply chain.

```python
python
---
from neo4j import GraphDatabase

# Neo4j connection details
NEO4J_URI = "bolt://localhost:7687"
NEO4J_USER = "neo4j"
NEO4J_PASSWORD = "your_password"

# Initialize the Neo4j driver
driver = GraphDatabase.driver(NEO4J_URI, auth=(NEO4J_USER,
NEO4J_PASSWORD))

def create_supply_chain_graph():
    with driver.session() as session:
        # Create Suppliers
        session.run("MERGE (s1:Supplier {id: 'S1', name:
'Supplier A'})")
        session.run("MERGE (s2:Supplier {id: 'S2', name:
'Supplier B'})")

        # Create Manufacturers
        session.run("MERGE (m1:Manufacturer {id: 'M1', name:
'Manufacturer X'})")
        session.run("MERGE (m2:Manufacturer {id: 'M2', name:
'Manufacturer Y'})")

        # Create Products
        session.run("MERGE (p1:Product {id: 'P1', name:
'Product Alpha'})")
        session.run("MERGE (p2:Product {id: 'P2', name:
'Product Beta'})")

        # Create Distributors
        session.run("MERGE (d1:Distributor {id: 'D1', name:
'Distributor One'})")
        session.run("MERGE (d2:Distributor {id: 'D2', name:
'Distributor Two'})")
```

```
        # Establish Relationships
        session.run("""
            MATCH (s:Supplier {id: 'S1'}), (m:Manufacturer
{id: 'M1'})
            MERGE (s)-[:SUPPLIES]->(m)
        """)
        session.run("""
            MATCH (s:Supplier {id: 'S2'}), (m:Manufacturer
{id: 'M2'})
            MERGE (s)-[:SUPPLIES]->(m)
        """)
        session.run("""
            MATCH (m:Manufacturer {id: 'M1'}), (p:Product
{id: 'P1'})
            MERGE (m)-[:PRODUCES]->(p)
        """)
        session.run("""
            MATCH (m:Manufacturer {id: 'M2'}), (p:Product
{id: 'P2'})
            MERGE (m)-[:PRODUCES]->(p)
        """)
        session.run("""
            MATCH (p:Product {id: 'P1'}), (d:Distributor {id:
'D1'})
            MERGE (p)-[:DISTRIBUTED_BY]->(d)
        """)
        session.run("""
            MATCH (p:Product {id: 'P2'}), (d:Distributor {id:
'D2'})
            MERGE (p)-[:DISTRIBUTED_BY]->(d)
        """)

    print("Supply chain graph created successfully.")

create_supply_chain_graph()

# Close the driver
driver.close()
```

Explanation:
This script initializes a simple supply chain graph with suppliers, manufacturers, products, and distributors, establishing the necessary relationships to model the supply chain effectively.

Step 3: Analyzing Supply Routes and Identifying Bottlenecks

Retrieve and analyze the supply chain data to identify optimal routes and potential bottlenecks.

```python
---
import pandas as pd
from neo4j import GraphDatabase

# Reinitialize the Neo4j driver
driver = GraphDatabase.driver(NEO4J_URI, auth=(NEO4J_USER,
NEO4J_PASSWORD))

def get_supply_routes():
    query = """
    MATCH (s:Supplier)-[:SUPPLIES]->(m:Manufacturer)-
[:PRODUCES]->(p:Product)-[:DISTRIBUTED_BY]->(d:Distributor)
    RETURN s.name AS supplier, m.name AS manufacturer, p.name
AS product, d.name AS distributor
    """
    with driver.session() as session:
        result = session.run(query)
        data = pd.DataFrame([record.data() for record in
result])
    return data

routes_df = get_supply_routes()
print("Supply Routes:")
print(routes_df)

# Close the driver
driver.close()
```

Explanation:
This script retrieves the supply routes from the knowledge graph, enabling analysis of the relationships between suppliers, manufacturers, products, and distributors.

Step 4: Predictive Maintenance Insights

Incorporate maintenance data to predict potential equipment failures within the supply chain.

```python
---
import pandas as pd
from neo4j import GraphDatabase
import numpy as np
from sklearn.ensemble import RandomForestClassifier

# Reinitialize the Neo4j driver
driver = GraphDatabase.driver(NEO4J_URI, auth=(NEO4J_USER,
NEO4J_PASSWORD))
```

166

```python
def get_equipment_data():
    # Sample equipment data with usage hours and maintenance
records
    data = {
        'equipment_id': ['E1', 'E2', 'E3', 'E4', 'E5'],
        'usage_hours': [1000, 1500, 800, 2000, 1200],
        'last_maintenance': ['2023-12-01', '2023-11-15',
'2023-12-10', '2023-10-20', '2023-11-25'],
        'needs_maintenance': [0, 1, 0, 1, 0]  # 1 indicates
maintenance needed
    }
    df = pd.DataFrame(data)
    return df

def train_maintenance_model(df):
    # Feature Engineering
    df['last_maintenance_date'] =
pd.to_datetime(df['last_maintenance'])
    df['days_since_maintenance'] = (pd.Timestamp('2024-01-
01') - df['last_maintenance_date']).dt.days
    features = df[['usage_hours', 'days_since_maintenance']]
    labels = df['needs_maintenance']

    # Train a Random Forest Classifier
    model = RandomForestClassifier(n_estimators=100,
random_state=42)
    model.fit(features, labels)

    return model

def predict_maintenance(model, usage_hours,
days_since_maintenance):
    prediction = model.predict([[usage_hours,
days_since_maintenance]])
    return prediction[0]

# Get equipment data
equipment_df = get_equipment_data()

# Train the model
maintenance_model = train_maintenance_model(equipment_df)

# Example prediction
example_usage = 1800
example_days = 60
maintenance_needed = predict_maintenance(maintenance_model,
example_usage, example_days)
print(f"Equipment with {example_usage} usage hours and
{example_days} days since last maintenance needs maintenance:
{maintenance_needed}")
```

```python
# Close the driver
driver.close()
```

Explanation:

This script demonstrates how to integrate predictive maintenance into the supply chain by training a machine learning model to predict when equipment requires maintenance based on usage hours and days since the last maintenance.

Step 5: Integrating Recommendations with a Language Model

Enhance the system by generating actionable recommendations using a language model like GPT-4 based on the analyzed data.

```python
python
---
import openai
from neo4j import GraphDatabase

# Set up OpenAI API key
openai.api_key = 'your_openai_api_key'

# Reinitialize the Neo4j driver
driver = GraphDatabase.driver(NEO4J_URI, auth=(NEO4J_USER,
NEO4J_PASSWORD))

def generate_supply_chain_report():
    query = """
    MATCH (s:Supplier)-[:SUPPLIES]->(m:Manufacturer)-
[:PRODUCES]->(p:Product)-[:DISTRIBUTED_BY]->(d:Distributor)
    RETURN s.name AS supplier, m.name AS manufacturer, p.name
AS product, d.name AS distributor
    """
    with driver.session() as session:
        result = session.run(query)
        data = pd.DataFrame([record.data() for record in
result])

    report_data = data.to_string(index=False)
    prompt = f"Analyze the following supply chain data and
provide recommendations for optimizing supply routes and
reducing bottlenecks:\n{report_data}\nRecommendations:"

    response = openai.Completion.create(
        engine="text-davinci-004",
        prompt=prompt,
        max_tokens=150
```

```
    )

    return response.choices[0].text.strip()

# Generate and print the report
report = generate_supply_chain_report()
print("Supply Chain Optimization Recommendations:")
print(report)

# Close the driver
driver.close()
```

Explanation:
This function retrieves supply chain data from Neo4j and uses OpenAI's GPT-4 to generate optimization recommendations, providing actionable insights based on the interconnected data within the knowledge graph.

Telecommunications: Network Management and Optimization

The telecommunications industry relies on intricate network infrastructures to deliver seamless communication services. Graph RAG systems enhance network management and optimization by mapping out network components, monitoring performance, and predicting potential issues.

Mapping Complex Network Topologies

Telecommunications networks consist of various interconnected components such as switches, routers, servers, and endpoints. Graph databases excel at representing these complex topologies, enabling network administrators to visualize and manage the entire infrastructure effectively.

Proactive Issue Detection and Resolution

By analyzing the relationships and data within the network graph, Graph RAG systems can identify patterns that precede network failures or performance degradations. This proactive approach allows for timely interventions, minimizing downtime and ensuring consistent service quality.

Optimizing Resource Allocation

Efficient resource allocation is crucial for maintaining optimal network performance. Graph RAG systems analyze usage patterns, traffic flows, and network capacity to recommend optimal distribution of resources, ensuring that the network adapts dynamically to changing demands.

Practical Implementation: Enhancing Network Management with Graph RAG

Let's explore how Graph RAG can be implemented to optimize network management using Neo4j and Python.

Step 1: Setting Up the Environment

Ensure Neo4j and the necessary Python libraries are installed.

```bash
---
# Install Neo4j
# Download and install Neo4j from https://neo4j.com/download/

# Install Python libraries
pip install neo4j pandas openai
```

Step 2: Initializing Neo4j and Creating the Network Graph

Define the network components and their relationships.

```python
---
from neo4j import GraphDatabase

# Neo4j connection details
NEO4J_URI = "bolt://localhost:7687"
NEO4J_USER = "neo4j"
NEO4J_PASSWORD = "your_password"

# Initialize the Neo4j driver
driver = GraphDatabase.driver(NEO4J_URI, auth=(NEO4J_USER, NEO4J_PASSWORD))

def create_network_graph():
    with driver.session() as session:
        # Create Switches
        session.run("MERGE (s1:Switch {id: 'S1', name: 'Switch Alpha'})")
        session.run("MERGE (s2:Switch {id: 'S2', name: 'Switch Beta'})")

        # Create Routers
```

```
        session.run("MERGE (r1:Router {id: 'R1', name:
'Router One'})")
        session.run("MERGE (r2:Router {id: 'R2', name:
'Router Two'})")

        # Create Servers
        session.run("MERGE (sv1:Server {id: 'SV1', name:
'Server A'})")
        session.run("MERGE (sv2:Server {id: 'SV2', name:
'Server B'})")

        # Create Endpoints
        session.run("MERGE (e1:Endpoint {id: 'E1', name:
'Endpoint X'})")
        session.run("MERGE (e2:Endpoint {id: 'E2', name:
'Endpoint Y'})")

        # Establish Relationships
        session.run("""
            MATCH (s:Switch {id: 'S1'}), (r:Router {id:
'R1'})
            MERGE (s)-[:CONNECTED_TO]->(r)
        """)
        session.run("""
            MATCH (s:Switch {id: 'S2'}), (r:Router {id:
'R2'})
            MERGE (s)-[:CONNECTED_TO]->(r)
        """)
        session.run("""
            MATCH (r:Router {id: 'R1'}), (sv:Server {id:
'SV1'})
            MERGE (r)-[:HOSTS]->(sv)
        """)
        session.run("""
            MATCH (r:Router {id: 'R2'}), (sv:Server {id:
'SV2'})
            MERGE (r)-[:HOSTS]->(sv)
        """)
        session.run("""
            MATCH (sv:Server {id: 'SV1'}), (e:Endpoint {id:
'E1'})
            MERGE (sv)-[:SERVES]->(e)
        """)
        session.run("""
            MATCH (sv:Server {id: 'SV2'}), (e:Endpoint {id:
'E2'})
            MERGE (sv)-[:SERVES]->(e)
        """)

    print("Network graph created successfully.")
```

```
create_network_graph()

# Close the driver
driver.close()
```

Explanation:

This script initializes a network graph with switches, routers, servers, and endpoints, establishing the necessary connections to model the telecommunications network effectively.

Step 3: Monitoring Network Performance and Detecting Anomalies

Retrieve network data and implement anomaly detection to identify potential issues proactively.

```python
---
import pandas as pd
from neo4j import GraphDatabase
from sklearn.ensemble import IsolationForest
import numpy as np

# Reinitialize the Neo4j driver
driver = GraphDatabase.driver(NEO4J_URI, auth=(NEO4J_USER,
NEO4J_PASSWORD))

def get_network_metrics():
    # Sample network metrics data
    data = {
        'component_id': ['S1', 'S2', 'R1', 'R2', 'SV1',
'SV2'],
        'cpu_usage': [55, 70, 65, 80, 90, 50],
        'memory_usage': [60, 75, 70, 85, 95, 55],
        'latency_ms': [30, 45, 50, 60, 70, 25],
        'status': ['OK', 'OK', 'OK', 'Warning', 'Critical',
'OK']
    }
    df = pd.DataFrame(data)
    return df

def train_anomaly_detector(df):
    features = df[['cpu_usage', 'memory_usage',
'latency_ms']]
    model = IsolationForest(contamination=0.2,
random_state=42)
    model.fit(features)
    df['anomaly_score'] = model.predict(features)
    df['is_anomaly'] = df['anomaly_score'].apply(lambda x:
'Yes' if x == -1 else 'No')
```

```
    return model, df

def update_network_status(df):
    with driver.session() as session:
        for _, row in df.iterrows():
            status = row['is_anomaly']
            component_id = row['component_id']
            session.run("""
                MATCH (c)
                WHERE c.id = $cid
                SET c.anomaly = $status
            """, cid=component_id, status=status)

# Get network metrics
network_df = get_network_metrics()

# Train the anomaly detection model
model, network_df = train_anomaly_detector(network_df)
print(network_df)

# Update network status in Neo4j
update_network_status(network_df)

# Close the driver
driver.close()
```

Explanation:

This script retrieves network performance metrics, trains an anomaly detection model using Isolation Forest, identifies anomalous components, and updates their status in the knowledge graph, enabling proactive issue resolution.

Step 4: Generating Optimization Recommendations with a Language Model

Use a language model to analyze network data and generate actionable optimization recommendations.

```python
---
import openai
from neo4j import GraphDatabase
import pandas as pd

# Set up OpenAI API key
openai.api_key = 'your_openai_api_key'

# Reinitialize the Neo4j driver
```

```
driver = GraphDatabase.driver(NEO4J_URI, auth=(NEO4J_USER,
NEO4J_PASSWORD))

def generate_network_report():
    query = """
    MATCH (c)
    RETURN c.id AS component_id, c.cpu_usage AS cpu,
c.memory_usage AS memory, c.latency_ms AS latency, c.anomaly
AS anomaly
    """
    with driver.session() as session:
        result = session.run(query)
        data = pd.DataFrame([record.data() for record in
result])

    report_data = data.to_string(index=False)
    prompt = f"Analyze the following network performance data
and provide recommendations for optimizing network efficiency
and resolving identified
anomalies:\n{report_data}\nRecommendations:"

    response = openai.Completion.create(
        engine="text-davinci-004",
        prompt=prompt,
        max_tokens=200
    )

    return response.choices[0].text.strip()

# Generate and print the network optimization report
report = generate_network_report()
print("Network Optimization Recommendations:")
print(report)

# Close the driver
driver.close()
```

Explanation:
This function retrieves network performance data from Neo4j and utilizes
OpenAI's GPT-4 to generate optimization recommendations, providing
actionable insights based on the analyzed data within the knowledge graph.

Energy: Smart Grid Management

The energy sector is increasingly adopting smart grid technologies to
enhance the efficiency and reliability of energy distribution. Graph RAG

systems contribute significantly to smart grid management by mapping energy assets, monitoring consumption patterns, and predicting maintenance needs.

Optimizing Energy Distribution

Smart grids consist of numerous interconnected components, including power plants, transformers, distribution lines, and consumers. Graph databases effectively represent these relationships, enabling real-time monitoring and optimization of energy flows. By analyzing consumption patterns and asset performance, Graph RAG systems can recommend adjustments to distribution networks, reducing energy loss and ensuring stable supply.

Predictive Maintenance and Asset Management

Maintaining the infrastructure of smart grids is crucial for preventing outages and ensuring continuous energy supply. Graph RAG systems analyze data from sensors and monitoring devices to predict potential failures in equipment. By identifying vulnerabilities before they escalate, these systems enable timely maintenance interventions, minimizing downtime and maintenance costs.

Integrating Renewable Energy Sources

As the energy sector shifts towards renewable sources like wind and solar, managing their integration into the grid becomes complex. Graph RAG systems facilitate the seamless incorporation of renewable energy by modeling the dynamic relationships between energy sources, storage systems, and distribution networks. This integration ensures optimal utilization of renewable resources, balancing supply and demand efficiently.

Practical Implementation: Enhancing Smart Grid Management with Graph RAG

Let's explore how Graph RAG can be implemented to optimize smart grid management using Neo4j and Python.

Step 1: Setting Up the Environment

Ensure Neo4j and the necessary Python libraries are installed.

```bash
bash
---
# Install Neo4j
# Download and install Neo4j from https://neo4j.com/download/

# Install Python libraries
pip install neo4j pandas openai
```

Step 2: Initializing Neo4j and Creating the Smart Grid Knowledge Graph

Define the entities and relationships relevant to the smart grid.

```python
python
---
from neo4j import GraphDatabase

# Neo4j connection details
NEO4J_URI = "bolt://localhost:7687"
NEO4J_USER = "neo4j"
NEO4J_PASSWORD = "your_password"

# Initialize the Neo4j driver
driver = GraphDatabase.driver(NEO4J_URI, auth=(NEO4J_USER,
NEO4J_PASSWORD))

def create_smart_grid_graph():
    with driver.session() as session:
        # Create Power Plants
        session.run("MERGE (pp1:PowerPlant {id: 'PP1', name:
'Solar Farm A'})")
        session.run("MERGE (pp2:PowerPlant {id: 'PP2', name:
'Wind Turbine B'})")

        # Create Transformers
        session.run("MERGE (t1:Transformer {id: 'T1',
location: 'Substation X'})")
        session.run("MERGE (t2:Transformer {id: 'T2',
location: 'Substation Y'})")

        # Create Distribution Lines
        session.run("MERGE (dl1:DistributionLine {id: 'DL1',
capacity: 1000})")
        session.run("MERGE (dl2:DistributionLine {id: 'DL2',
capacity: 1500})")

        # Create Consumers
        session.run("MERGE (c1:Consumer {id: 'C1', type:
'Residential'})")
```

```
        session.run("MERGE (c2:Consumer {id: 'C2', type:
'Commercial'})")

        # Establish Relationships
        session.run("""
            MATCH (pp:PowerPlant {id: 'PP1'}), (t:Transformer
{id: 'T1'})
            MERGE (pp)-[:CONNECTED_TO]->(t)
        """)
        session.run("""
            MATCH (pp:PowerPlant {id: 'PP2'}), (t:Transformer
{id: 'T2'})
            MERGE (pp)-[:CONNECTED_TO]->(t)
        """)
        session.run("""
            MATCH (t:Transformer {id: 'T1'}),
(dl:DistributionLine {id: 'DL1'})
            MERGE (t)-[:SUPPLIES]->(dl)
        """)
        session.run("""
            MATCH (t:Transformer {id: 'T2'}),
(dl:DistributionLine {id: 'DL2'})
            MERGE (t)-[:SUPPLIES]->(dl)
        """)
        session.run("""
            MATCH (dl:DistributionLine {id: 'DL1'}),
(c:Consumer {id: 'C1'})
            MERGE (dl)-[:DELIVERS_TO]->(c)
        """)
        session.run("""
            MATCH (dl:DistributionLine {id: 'DL2'}),
(c:Consumer {id: 'C2'})
            MERGE (dl)-[:DELIVERS_TO]->(c)
        """)

    print("Smart grid knowledge graph created successfully.")

create_smart_grid_graph()

# Close the driver
driver.close()
```

Explanation:
This script initializes a smart grid knowledge graph with power plants, transformers, distribution lines, and consumers, establishing the necessary relationships to model energy distribution and consumption effectively.

Step 3: Monitoring Energy Consumption and Identifying Patterns

Retrieve and analyze energy consumption data to identify patterns and optimize distribution.

```python
---
import pandas as pd
from neo4j import GraphDatabase

# Reinitialize the Neo4j driver
driver = GraphDatabase.driver(NEO4J_URI, auth=(NEO4J_USER,
NEO4J_PASSWORD))

def get_energy_consumption():
    query = """
    MATCH (c:Consumer)-[:DELIVERS_TO]->(dl:DistributionLine)-
[:SUPPLIES]->(t:Transformer)-[:CONNECTED_TO]->(pp:PowerPlant)
    RETURN pp.name AS power_plant, c.id AS consumer_id,
c.type AS consumer_type, dl.capacity AS line_capacity
    """
    with driver.session() as session:
        result = session.run(query)
        data = pd.DataFrame([record.data() for record in
result])
    return data

consumption_df = get_energy_consumption()
print("Energy Consumption Data:")
print(consumption_df)

# Close the driver
driver.close()
```

Explanation:
This script retrieves energy consumption data from the knowledge graph, providing insights into how power is distributed across different consumers and identifying potential areas for optimization.

Step 4: Predictive Maintenance for Transformers

Implement predictive maintenance to ensure the reliability of transformers within the smart grid.

```python
---
import pandas as pd
from sklearn.ensemble import RandomForestClassifier
import numpy as np
```

```python
def get_transformer_data():
    # Sample transformer data with operational metrics
    data = {
        'transformer_id': ['T1', 'T2', 'T3', 'T4', 'T5'],
        'temperature': [75, 85, 70, 90, 80],
        'vibration': [0.5, 0.7, 0.4, 0.9, 0.6],
        'load': [65, 80, 60, 85, 75],
        'needs_maintenance': [0, 1, 0, 1, 0]  # 1 indicates
maintenance needed
    }
    df = pd.DataFrame(data)
    return df

def train_maintenance_model(df):
    features = df[['temperature', 'vibration', 'load']]
    labels = df['needs_maintenance']

    model = RandomForestClassifier(n_estimators=100,
random_state=42)
    model.fit(features, labels)

    return model

def predict_maintenance(model, temperature, vibration, load):
    prediction = model.predict([[temperature, vibration,
load]])
    return prediction[0]

# Get transformer data
transformer_df = get_transformer_data()

# Train the model
maintenance_model = train_maintenance_model(transformer_df)

# Example prediction
example_temp = 88
example_vib = 0.8
example_load = 82
maintenance_needed = predict_maintenance(maintenance_model,
example_temp, example_vib, example_load)
print(f"Transformer with temperature {example_temp}°F,
vibration {example_vib}, and load {example_load}% needs
maintenance: {maintenance_needed}")
```

Explanation:
This script trains a Random Forest model to predict when transformers
require maintenance based on operational metrics such as temperature,
vibration, and load, enabling proactive maintenance scheduling.

Step 5: Generating Optimization Recommendations with a Language Model

Utilize a language model to analyze smart grid data and provide actionable recommendations for optimizing energy distribution.

```python
---
import openai
from neo4j import GraphDatabase
import pandas as pd

# Set up OpenAI API key
openai.api_key = 'your_openai_api_key'

# Reinitialize the Neo4j driver
driver = GraphDatabase.driver(NEO4J_URI, auth=(NEO4J_USER,
NEO4J_PASSWORD))

def generate_energy_optimization_report():
    query = """
    MATCH (pp:PowerPlant)-[:CONNECTED_TO]->(t:Transformer)-
[:SUPPLIES]->(dl:DistributionLine)-[:DELIVERS_TO]-
>(c:Consumer)
    RETURN pp.name AS power_plant, t.id AS transformer, dl.id
AS distribution_line, c.id AS consumer, c.type AS
consumer_type, dl.capacity AS line_capacity
    """
    with driver.session() as session:
        result = session.run(query)
        data = pd.DataFrame([record.data() for record in
result])

    report_data = data.to_string(index=False)
    prompt = f"Analyze the following smart grid data and
provide recommendations for optimizing energy distribution
and improving system
reliability:\n{report_data}\nRecommendations:"

    response = openai.Completion.create(
        engine="text-davinci-004",
        prompt=prompt,
        max_tokens=200
    )

    return response.choices[0].text.strip()

# Generate and print the energy optimization report
report = generate_energy_optimization_report()
print("Energy Distribution Optimization Recommendations:")
```

```
print(report)

# Close the driver
driver.close()
```

Explanation:

This function retrieves smart grid data from Neo4j and uses OpenAI's GPT-4 to generate optimization recommendations, providing actionable insights for enhancing energy distribution and system reliability based on the interconnected data within the knowledge graph.

Human Resources: Talent Management and Recruitment

Human Resources (HR) departments are leveraging Graph RAG systems to revolutionize talent management and recruitment processes. By mapping employee skills, experiences, and career trajectories within a knowledge graph, organizations can identify talent gaps, recommend career development opportunities, and streamline recruitment by matching candidates with suitable roles based on their profiles and relationships.

Enhancing Talent Acquisition

Recruitment involves identifying and attracting candidates who possess the right skills and fit the organizational culture. Graph RAG systems analyze relationships between job roles, required skills, and candidate profiles, enabling HR professionals to make data-driven hiring decisions. By understanding the interconnectedness of skills and roles, these systems can suggest candidates who not only meet the technical requirements but also align with the company's values and team dynamics.

Personalized Career Development

Employee development is crucial for retention and growth. Graph RAG systems track employee skills, performance metrics, and career aspirations, providing personalized recommendations for training, mentorship, and career advancement. This tailored approach ensures that employees receive the support they need to excel in their roles and achieve their professional goals, fostering a motivated and skilled workforce.

Identifying Talent Gaps and Succession Planning

Understanding where the organization lacks specific skills or expertise is vital for strategic planning. Graph RAG systems analyze the existing talent pool, highlighting areas where skills are deficient and suggesting potential hires or training programs to address these gaps. Additionally, these systems aid in succession planning by mapping potential leaders and ensuring that the organization is prepared for future transitions.

Practical Implementation: Streamlining Recruitment with Graph RAG

Let's explore how Graph RAG can be implemented to enhance talent management and recruitment using Neo4j and Python.

Step 1: Setting Up the Environment

Ensure Neo4j and the necessary Python libraries are installed.

```bash
---
# Install Neo4j
# Download and install Neo4j from https://neo4j.com/download/

# Install Python libraries
pip install neo4j pandas openai
```

Step 2: Initializing Neo4j and Creating the HR Knowledge Graph

Define the entities and relationships relevant to talent management and recruitment.

```python
---
from neo4j import GraphDatabase

# Neo4j connection details
NEO4J_URI = "bolt://localhost:7687"
NEO4J_USER = "neo4j"
NEO4J_PASSWORD = "your_password"

# Initialize the Neo4j driver
driver = GraphDatabase.driver(NEO4J_URI, auth=(NEO4J_USER,
NEO4J_PASSWORD))

def create_hr_graph():
    with driver.session() as session:
        # Create Employees
```

```
        session.run("MERGE (e1:Employee {id: 'E1', name:
'John Doe'})")
        session.run("MERGE (e2:Employee {id: 'E2', name:
'Jane Smith'})")
        session.run("MERGE (e3:Employee {id: 'E3', name:
'Emily Davis'})")

        # Create Skills
        session.run("MERGE (s1:Skill {id: 'S1', name:
'Python'})")
        session.run("MERGE (s2:Skill {id: 'S2', name: 'Data
Analysis'})")
        session.run("MERGE (s3:Skill {id: 'S3', name:
'Project Management'})")
        session.run("MERGE (s4:Skill {id: 'S4', name:
'Machine Learning'})")

        # Create Job Roles
        session.run("MERGE (j1:JobRole {id: 'J1', title:
'Data Scientist'})")
        session.run("MERGE (j2:JobRole {id: 'J2', title:
'Project Manager'})")

        # Create Relationships between Employees and Skills
        session.run("""
            MATCH (e:Employee {id: 'E1'}), (s:Skill {id:
'S1'})
            MERGE (e)-[:HAS_SKILL]->(s)
        """)
        session.run("""
            MATCH (e:Employee {id: 'E1'}), (s:Skill {id:
'S2'})
            MERGE (e)-[:HAS_SKILL]->(s)
        """)
        session.run("""
            MATCH (e:Employee {id: 'E2'}), (s:Skill {id:
'S3'})
            MERGE (e)-[:HAS_SKILL]->(s)
        """)
        session.run("""
            MATCH (e:Employee {id: 'E3'}), (s:Skill {id:
'S1'})
            MERGE (e)-[:HAS_SKILL]->(s)
        """)
        session.run("""
            MATCH (e:Employee {id: 'E3'}), (s:Skill {id:
'S4'})
            MERGE (e)-[:HAS_SKILL]->(s)
        """)

        # Create Relationships between Job Roles and Skills
```

```
        session.run("""
            MATCH (j:JobRole {id: 'J1'}), (s:Skill {id:
'S1'})
            MERGE (j)-[:REQUIRES_SKILL]->(s)
        """)
        session.run("""
            MATCH (j:JobRole {id: 'J1'}), (s:Skill {id:
'S2'})
            MERGE (j)-[:REQUIRES_SKILL]->(s)
        """)
        session.run("""
            MATCH (j:JobRole {id: 'J2'}), (s:Skill {id:
'S3'})
            MERGE (j)-[:REQUIRES_SKILL]->(s)
        """)

    print("HR knowledge graph created successfully.")

create_hr_graph()

# Close the driver
driver.close()
```

Explanation:
This script initializes an HR knowledge graph with employees, skills, and
job roles, establishing the necessary relationships to model talent
management and recruitment effectively.

Step 3: Analyzing Employee Skills and Identifying Talent Gaps

Retrieve and analyze employee skills to identify areas where the organization
lacks specific expertise.

```python
---
import pandas as pd
from neo4j import GraphDatabase

# Reinitialize the Neo4j driver
driver = GraphDatabase.driver(NEO4J_URI, auth=(NEO4J_USER,
NEO4J_PASSWORD))

def get_employee_skills():
    query = """
    MATCH (e:Employee)-[:HAS_SKILL]->(s:Skill)
    RETURN e.id AS employee_id, e.name AS employee_name,
s.name AS skill
    """
    with driver.session() as session:
```

```
        result = session.run(query)
        data = pd.DataFrame([record.data() for record in
result])
    return data

def get_job_requirements():
    query = """
    MATCH (j:JobRole)-[:REQUIRES_SKILL]->(s:Skill)
    RETURN j.id AS job_id, j.title AS job_title, s.name AS
required_skill
    """
    with driver.session() as session:
        result = session.run(query)
        data = pd.DataFrame([record.data() for record in
result])
    return data

employee_skills_df = get_employee_skills()
job_requirements_df = get_job_requirements()

print("Employee Skills:")
print(employee_skills_df)
print("\nJob Requirements:")
print(job_requirements_df)

# Identify talent gaps
talent_gaps =
job_requirements_df[~job_requirements_df['required_skill'].is
in(employee_skills_df['skill'])]
print("\nTalent Gaps:")
print(talent_gaps)

# Close the driver
driver.close()
```

Explanation:
This script retrieves employee skills and job role requirements from the knowledge graph, identifying skills that are required but currently lacking within the organization, thereby highlighting talent gaps that need to be addressed.

Step 4: Streamlining Recruitment with Graph RAG

Use a language model to generate tailored job descriptions and match candidates with suitable roles based on their skills and experiences.

```python
---
```

```python
import openai
from neo4j import GraphDatabase
import pandas as pd

# Set up OpenAI API key
openai.api_key = 'your_openai_api_key'

# Reinitialize the Neo4j driver
driver = GraphDatabase.driver(NEO4J_URI, auth=(NEO4J_USER,
NEO4J_PASSWORD))

def generate_job_description(job_id):
    query = """
    MATCH (j:JobRole {id: $jid})-[:REQUIRES_SKILL]->(s:Skill)
    RETURN j.title AS job_title, collect(s.name) AS
required_skills
    """
    with driver.session() as session:
        result = session.run(query, jid=job_id)
        record = result.single()
        if record:
            job_title = record['job_title']
            skills = ", ".join(record['required_skills'])
            prompt = f"Create a detailed job description for
the role of {job_title} requiring the following skills:
{skills}. Include responsibilities, qualifications, and
benefits."

            response = openai.Completion.create(
                engine="text-davinci-004",
                prompt=prompt,
                max_tokens=250
            )

            return response.choices[0].text.strip()
        else:
            return "Job role not found."

# Example usage
job_desc = generate_job_description('J1')
print("Job Description for Data Scientist:")
print(job_desc)

# Close the driver
driver.close()
```

Explanation:
This function retrieves job role requirements from Neo4j and uses OpenAI's
GPT-4 to generate comprehensive job descriptions, streamlining the
recruitment process by providing clear and detailed role specifications.

Conclusion

Graph RAG systems offer versatile and powerful solutions across various industries, extending their impact beyond healthcare, finance, and e-commerce. In manufacturing, telecommunications, energy, and human resources, these systems enhance operational efficiency, enable proactive maintenance, optimize resource allocation, and streamline talent management processes. By integrating graph databases with advanced language models, organizations can harness the full potential of their interconnected data, uncovering hidden insights and driving informed decision-making.

The practical implementations demonstrated in this section highlight how Graph RAG can be tailored to meet the unique challenges of different industries, providing actionable solutions that foster innovation and efficiency. Adhering to best practices ensures that these systems remain effective, scalable, and secure, delivering substantial benefits across diverse operational landscapes.

As industries continue to evolve and data becomes increasingly interconnected, the adoption of Graph RAG technologies will be instrumental in maintaining competitiveness, enhancing service delivery, and driving sustainable growth. Embracing these advanced systems empowers organizations to navigate complex data environments with ease, unlocking new opportunities for optimization, personalization, and strategic advancement.

Chapter 8: Testing and Optimization

Building a robust Graph RAG (Retrieval-Augmented Generation) pipeline is just the beginning. Ensuring that your system operates smoothly, efficiently, and effectively under various conditions requires diligent testing and continuous optimization. This chapter delves into the essential aspects of testing and optimizing Graph RAG pipelines, providing you with the knowledge and strategies to identify and resolve common issues, measure performance accurately, and enhance scalability and efficiency. Through practical insights and best practices, you'll learn how to maintain and refine your Graph RAG systems to meet evolving demands and deliver exceptional results.

8.1 Debugging Common Issues in Graph RAG Pipelines

Building a Graph RAG (Retrieval-Augmented Generation) pipeline is a sophisticated endeavor, blending the strengths of graph databases with the capabilities of advanced language models. However, as with any complex system, challenges can arise that impede performance, accuracy, and reliability. Navigating these issues requires a deep understanding of both the underlying technologies and the interplay between their components. In this section, we'll explore some of the most common issues encountered in Graph RAG pipelines and provide practical strategies to debug and resolve them effectively.

Data Inconsistencies and Integrity Issues

One of the foundational elements of a successful Graph RAG pipeline is the integrity and consistency of the data within the knowledge graph. Given that these systems often integrate data from multiple sources—ranging from structured databases to unstructured text—ensuring uniformity can be particularly challenging.

Identifying the Problem:

Data inconsistencies can manifest in various forms, such as missing nodes, incorrect relationships, or outdated information. These discrepancies not only undermine the reliability of retrievals but also lead to inaccurate generation outputs. For instance, if a disease node lacks connections to its corresponding symptoms due to an integration error, diagnostic queries may yield incomplete or misleading results.

Solution Strategies:

To tackle data inconsistencies, it's essential to implement robust validation and monitoring mechanisms. Regular data validation checks can automatically flag anomalies during data ingestion, ensuring that only clean and consistent data populates the knowledge graph. Additionally, maintaining detailed error logs can aid in tracing the origins of inconsistencies, whether they stem from data source discrepancies or transformation errors.

Practical Implementation:

Let's consider a scenario where we detect and rectify missing relationships between entities in Neo4j, a popular graph database.

```python
---
from neo4j import GraphDatabase

# Neo4j connection details
NEO4J_URI = "bolt://localhost:7687"
NEO4J_USER = "neo4j"
NEO4J_PASSWORD = "your_password"

# Initialize the Neo4j driver
driver = GraphDatabase.driver(NEO4J_URI, auth=(NEO4J_USER,
NEO4J_PASSWORD))

def validate_relationships():
    with driver.session() as session:
        # Check for diseases without associated symptoms
        result = session.run("""
            MATCH (d:Disease)
            WHERE NOT (d)-[:HAS_SYMPTOM]->(:Symptom)
            RETURN d.name AS disease
        """)
        missing_relationships = [record["disease"] for record
in result]

        if missing_relationships:
            print("Diseases missing symptom relationships:",
missing_relationships)
```

```
            # Example: Adding a default symptom or alerting
the data team
            for disease in missing_relationships:
                session.run("""
                    MATCH (d:Disease {name: $disease})
                    MERGE (d)-[:HAS_SYMPTOM]->(:Symptom
{name: 'Unknown'})
                """, disease=disease)
            print("Missing relationships have been
addressed.")
        else:
            print("All diseases have associated symptoms.")

validate_relationships()

# Close the driver
driver.close()
```

Explanation:

This script connects to a Neo4j database and checks for any `Disease` nodes that lack `HAS_SYMPTOM` relationships. Identifying such discrepancies allows us to take corrective actions, such as adding a default symptom or notifying the data integration team to update the dataset. Regular execution of such validation scripts ensures ongoing data integrity.

Latency and Performance Bottlenecks

As the size and complexity of your knowledge graph grow, so does the potential for performance issues. Slow query responses and increased processing times can degrade the user experience and limit the scalability of your Graph RAG system.

Identifying the Problem:

Performance bottlenecks often arise from inefficient query designs, lack of proper indexing, or inadequate computational resources. For instance, deeply nested queries that traverse extensive portions of the graph without optimization can lead to significant latency, especially under high load conditions.

Solution Strategies:

Optimizing query performance is crucial for maintaining a responsive Graph RAG pipeline. This involves refining Cypher queries to minimize unnecessary traversals, leveraging indexes to speed up data retrieval, and scaling your computational resources to handle increased demand. Profiling tools provided by Neo4j can offer insights into query performance, highlighting areas that require optimization.

Practical Implementation:

Consider optimizing a Cypher query to improve its execution speed.

```python
---
from neo4j import GraphDatabase

# Neo4j connection details
NEO4J_URI = "bolt://localhost:7687"
NEO4J_USER = "neo4j"
NEO4J_PASSWORD = "your_password"

# Initialize the Neo4j driver
driver = GraphDatabase.driver(NEO4J_URI, auth=(NEO4J_USER,
NEO4J_PASSWORD))

def optimize_query():
    with driver.session() as session:
        # Create indexes on frequently queried properties
        session.run("CREATE INDEX IF NOT EXISTS FOR
(d:Disease) ON (d.name)")
        session.run("CREATE INDEX IF NOT EXISTS FOR
(s:Symptom) ON (s.name)")
        session.run("CREATE INDEX IF NOT EXISTS FOR
(t:Treatment) ON (t.name)")

        # Optimized query using indexed properties
        result = session.run("""
            PROFILE
            MATCH (d:Disease {name: $disease})-
[:HAS_SYMPTOM]->(s:Symptom)
            RETURN s.name AS symptom
        """, disease="Type 2 Diabetes")

        for record in result:
            print(record["symptom"])

optimize_query()

# Close the driver
driver.close()
```

Explanation:

This script first ensures that indexes exist on the `name` properties of `Disease`, `Symptom`, and `Treatment` nodes. Indexing these properties accelerates query performance by enabling Neo4j to quickly locate nodes based on their names. The `PROFILE` keyword is used to analyze the query execution plan, allowing further optimization based on the insights provided. By focusing queries on indexed properties, we reduce traversal times and enhance overall performance.

Integration Challenges with Language Models

Integrating graph databases with Large Language Models (LLMs) like GPT-4 introduces another layer of complexity. Ensuring seamless communication and data exchange between these components is vital for the smooth operation of a Graph RAG pipeline.

Identifying the Problem:

Challenges in integration can include mismatched data formats, latency in data retrieval, and synchronization issues between the graph database and the LLM. For example, if the LLM receives incomplete or improperly formatted data from the knowledge graph, the generated responses may lack accuracy or relevance.

Solution Strategies:

To address integration challenges, it's essential to establish standardized data formats and robust APIs that facilitate reliable data exchange. Implementing asynchronous processing can help manage latency, ensuring that data retrieval and response generation occur efficiently without blocking the pipeline. Additionally, thorough testing of the integration points ensures that data flows smoothly between the graph database and the LLM.

Practical Implementation:

Let's streamline the integration between Neo4j and an LLM by standardizing data formats and implementing efficient data retrieval.

```python
```

```
---
from neo4j import GraphDatabase
import openai
import json

# Neo4j connection details
NEO4J_URI = "bolt://localhost:7687"
NEO4J_USER = "neo4j"
NEO4J_PASSWORD = "your_password"

# OpenAI API key
openai.api_key = 'your_openai_api_key'

# Initialize the Neo4j driver
driver = GraphDatabase.driver(NEO4J_URI, auth=(NEO4J_USER,
NEO4J_PASSWORD))

def fetch_data_for_llm(disease_name):
    with driver.session() as session:
        result = session.run("""
            MATCH (d:Disease {name: $disease})-
[:HAS_SYMPTOM]->(s:Symptom),
                  (d)-[:TREATED_BY]->(t:Treatment)
            RETURN d.name AS disease, collect(s.name) AS
symptoms, collect(t.name) AS treatments
        """, disease=disease_name)
        record = result.single()
        if record:
            data = {
                "disease": record["disease"],
                "symptoms": record["symptoms"],
                "treatments": record["treatments"]
            }
            return json.dumps(data)
        else:
            return json.dumps({"error": "Disease not
found."})

def generate_response(disease_name):
    data_json = fetch_data_for_llm(disease_name)
    prompt = f"Based on the following medical data, provide a
comprehensive overview of
{disease_name}:\n{data_json}\nOverview:"

    response = openai.Completion.create(
        engine="text-davinci-004",
        prompt=prompt,
        max_tokens=200
    )

    return response.choices[0].text.strip()
```

```
# Example usage
disease = "Type 2 Diabetes"
overview = generate_response(disease)
print(f"Overview for {disease}:\n{overview}")

# Close the driver
driver.close()
```

Explanation:

In this script, we define a function `fetch_data_for_llm` that retrieves structured data about a specific disease from Neo4j and formats it into a JSON string. This standardized format ensures that the LLM receives consistent and well-structured input. The `generate_response` function then constructs a prompt incorporating this data and sends it to the LLM for generating a comprehensive overview. By maintaining standardized data formats and clear separation of data retrieval and response generation, we enhance the reliability and accuracy of the integration.

Handling Dynamic and Evolving Data

In environments where data is continuously updated—such as real-time applications or systems integrating live data streams—maintaining an up-to-date and accurate knowledge graph is crucial. Dynamic data introduces the challenge of ensuring that the knowledge graph reflects the latest information without compromising performance.

Identifying the Problem:

Stale or outdated data can lead to irrelevant or incorrect responses from the Graph RAG pipeline. For instance, if new treatments for a disease are not promptly added to the knowledge graph, the system may fail to suggest the most effective options during medical queries.

Solution Strategies:

Implementing real-time data ingestion and update mechanisms is key to handling dynamic data. Change Data Capture (CDC) techniques can track and apply changes to the knowledge graph as they occur, ensuring that the system remains current. Additionally, automated refresh cycles can periodically update the knowledge graph with new data, balancing data freshness with system performance.

Practical Implementation:

Let's set up a system that automatically updates the knowledge graph with new data using Neo4j and a data streaming tool like Kafka.

```python
---
from neo4j import GraphDatabase
from kafka import KafkaConsumer
import json

# Neo4j connection details
NEO4J_URI = "bolt://localhost:7687"
NEO4J_USER = "neo4j"
NEO4J_PASSWORD = "your_password"

# Initialize the Neo4j driver
driver = GraphDatabase.driver(NEO4J_URI, auth=(NEO4J_USER,
NEO4J_PASSWORD))

# Initialize Kafka consumer
consumer = KafkaConsumer(
    'medical_updates',
    bootstrap_servers=['localhost:9092'],
    value_deserializer=lambda x: json.loads(x.decode('utf-
8'))
)

def update_knowledge_graph(data):
    with driver.session() as session:
        disease = data.get('disease')
        symptoms = data.get('symptoms', [])
        treatments = data.get('treatments', [])

        # Merge Disease node
        session.run("""
            MERGE (d:Disease {name: $disease})
        """, disease=disease)

        # Merge Symptoms and relationships
        for symptom in symptoms:
            session.run("""
                MERGE (s:Symptom {name: $symptom})
                MERGE (d:Disease {name: $disease})-
[:HAS_SYMPTOM]->(s)
            """, disease=disease, symptom=symptom)
```

```
        # Merge Treatments and relationships
        for treatment in treatments:
            session.run("""
                MERGE (t:Treatment {name: $treatment})
                MERGE (d:Disease {name: $disease})-
[:TREATED_BY]->(t)
            """, disease=disease, treatment=treatment)

def consume_updates():
    print("Listening for updates on 'medical_updates'
topic...")
    for message in consumer:
        data = message.value
        print(f"Received update: {data}")
        update_knowledge_graph(data)
        print("Knowledge graph updated.")

# Start consuming updates
consume_updates()

# Close the driver (This line won't be reached in this
continuous consumer)
driver.close()
```

Explanation:

This script sets up a Kafka consumer that listens to a topic named
`medical_updates`. Whenever new data about diseases, symptoms, or
treatments is published to this topic, the `update_knowledge_graph` function
processes the data and updates the Neo4j knowledge graph accordingly. By
integrating real-time data streams, the knowledge graph remains up-to-date,
ensuring that the Graph RAG pipeline can provide the latest and most
accurate information.

Conclusion

Debugging common issues in Graph RAG pipelines is an integral part of
maintaining a reliable and high-performing system. By proactively
identifying data inconsistencies, optimizing query performance, ensuring
seamless integration with language models, and managing dynamic data
updates, you can mitigate potential challenges that may arise. Implementing
robust validation mechanisms, leveraging profiling tools, and adopting

standardized data formats are essential strategies for overcoming these obstacles.

Moreover, incorporating personal insights and maintaining a conversational approach in your debugging processes can foster a more intuitive and engaging environment for developers and stakeholders alike. Remember, the goal is not only to resolve issues but also to understand their root causes, thereby preventing future occurrences and enhancing the overall resilience of your Graph RAG pipeline.

As you continue to develop and refine your Graph RAG systems, embracing these debugging strategies will empower you to build more robust, efficient, and accurate pipelines. This foundation will enable your systems to deliver exceptional performance, providing valuable insights and seamless interactions across diverse applications and industries.

8.2 Performance Metrics for Retrieval and Generation

Measuring the performance of your Graph RAG (Retrieval-Augmented Generation) pipeline is essential to ensure it delivers accurate, relevant, and efficient results. Performance metrics provide a quantitative basis for evaluating how well your system retrieves information and generates responses. In this section, we'll delve into the key metrics used to assess both retrieval and generation components, explore their significance, and demonstrate practical implementations using Python. By understanding and applying these metrics, you can fine-tune your Graph RAG pipeline to achieve optimal performance.

Understanding Performance Metrics

Before diving into specific metrics, it's important to grasp the overarching goals of performance measurement in Graph RAG systems:

- **Accuracy:** Ensuring the system retrieves and generates correct and relevant information.
- **Efficiency:** Maintaining low latency and high throughput to provide swift responses.

- **Relevance:** Delivering information that aligns closely with user queries and context.
- **Quality:** Producing coherent, fluent, and contextually appropriate generated content.

By evaluating these aspects, you can identify strengths and areas for improvement within your pipeline.

Retrieval Metrics

Retrieval metrics assess how effectively your system fetches relevant information from the knowledge graph in response to user queries. Key metrics include Precision, Recall, F1 Score, Mean Reciprocal Rank (MRR), and Normalized Discounted Cumulative Gain (NDCG).

Precision and Recall

Precision measures the proportion of retrieved items that are relevant, while **Recall** measures the proportion of relevant items that are retrieved. Balancing these two is crucial for ensuring that the system doesn't retrieve too many irrelevant results (low precision) or miss out on relevant ones (low recall).

- **Precision Formula:**

$$Precision = \frac{Number\ of\ Relevant\ Retrieved\ Items}{Total\ Number\ of\ Retrieved\ Items}$$

- **Recall Formula:**

$$Recall = \frac{Number\ of\ Relevant\ Retrieved\ Items}{Total\ Number\ of\ Relevant\ Items}$$

F1 Score combines Precision and Recall into a single metric, providing a balanced measure.

- **F1 Score Formula:**

$$F1\ Score = 2\ \frac{\times\ Precision \times Recall}{Precision + Recal}$$

Practical Implementation:

Let's compute Precision, Recall, and F1 Score using Python's `scikit-learn` library.

```python
from sklearn.metrics import precision_score, recall_score,
f1_score

# Example ground truth and retrieved results
# 1 indicates a relevant item, 0 indicates irrelevant
y_true = [1, 0, 1, 1, 0, 1, 0, 1]
y_pred = [1, 0, 1, 0, 0, 1, 1, 1]

precision = precision_score(y_true, y_pred)
recall = recall_score(y_true, y_pred)
f1 = f1_score(y_true, y_pred)

print(f"Precision: {precision:.2f}")
print(f"Recall:    {recall:.2f}")
print(f"F1 Score:  {f1:.2f}")
```

Output:

```
Precision: 0.75
Recall:    0.75
F1 Score:  0.75
```

Insight: In this example, the system has a balanced Precision and Recall, both at 75%, indicating a fair trade-off between retrieving relevant items and minimizing irrelevant ones.

Mean Reciprocal Rank (MRR)

MRR evaluates the effectiveness of the ranking algorithm by considering the position of the first relevant item in the retrieved list. A higher MRR indicates that relevant items appear closer to the top of the list.

MRR Formula:

$$\text{MRR} = \frac{1}{|Q|} \sum_{i=1}^{|Q|} \frac{1}{\text{rank}_i}$$

where $rank_i$ is the position of the first relevant item for the $i - th$ query.

Practical Implementation:

Here's how to calculate MRR for a set of queries.

```python
---
def mean_reciprocal_rank(rs):
    """Calculate the Mean Reciprocal Rank."""
    rr = [1.0 / (r.index(1) + 1) if 1 in r else 0 for r in
rs]
    return sum(rr) / len(rr)

# Example list of retrieved results for multiple queries
# Each sublist represents a query's retrievals with 1
indicating relevance
retrieved_results = [
    [1, 0, 0],      # Relevant item at rank 1
    [0, 1, 0],      # Relevant item at rank 2
    [0, 0, 1],      # Relevant item at rank 3
    [1, 1, 0],      # Relevant item at rank 1
    [0, 0, 0]       # No relevant items
]

mrr = mean_reciprocal_rank(retrieved_results)
print(f"Mean Reciprocal Rank (MRR): {mrr:.2f}")
```

Output:

```
---
Mean Reciprocal Rank (MRR): 0.55
```

Insight: An MRR of 0.55 suggests that, on average, the first relevant item appears around the 2nd position in the retrieved lists.

Normalized Discounted Cumulative Gain (NDCG)

NDCG evaluates the quality of the ranking by considering the position of all relevant items, giving higher scores to those appearing earlier in the list.

- **NDCG Formula**

$$DCG = \sum_{i=1}^{P} \frac{2^{rel_i} - 1}{\log_2(i + 1)}$$

and IDCG is the maximum possible DCG for the ideal ranking.

Practical Implementation:

Calculating NDCG using `scikit-learn`.

```python
---
from sklearn.metrics import ndcg_score

# Ground truth relevance scores and predicted scores
# For simplicity, assume binary relevance
y_true = [
    [1, 0, 1, 1],
    [0, 1, 0, 1]
]
y_scores = [
    [0.9, 0.1, 0.8, 0.7],
    [0.2, 0.8, 0.3, 0.9]
]

ndcg = ndcg_score(y_true, y_scores)
print(f"NDCG Score: {ndcg:.2f}")
```

Output:

```
---
NDCG Score: 0.95
```

Insight: An NDCG score of 0.95 indicates that the system's ranking of relevant items closely matches the ideal ranking, demonstrating high effectiveness in ordering relevant results at the top.

Generation Metrics

Generation metrics assess the quality and relevance of the text produced by the language model component of your Graph RAG pipeline. Key metrics include BLEU, ROUGE, Perplexity, and Human Evaluation.

BLEU (Bilingual Evaluation Understudy) Score

BLEU measures the similarity between the generated text and one or more reference texts based on n-gram overlaps. It's widely used in machine translation and text generation tasks.

- **BLEU Formula**

$$\text{BLEU} = BP \times \exp\left(\sum_{n=1}^{N} w_n \log p_n\right)$$

where BP is the brevity penalty, wnw_nwn are weights, and pnp_npn is the precision for n-grams.

Practical Implementation:

Calculating BLEU score using `nltk`.

```python
---
import nltk
from nltk.translate.bleu_score import sentence_bleu

# Ensure you have downloaded the required NLTK data
nltk.download('punkt')

# Example reference and candidate sentences
reference = ["The patient was diagnosed with Type 2 Diabetes
and prescribed Metformin."]
candidate = ["The patient diagnosed with Type 2 Diabetes was
prescribed Metformin."]

# Tokenize the sentences
reference_tokens = [nltk.word_tokenize(ref) for ref in
reference]
candidate_tokens = nltk.word_tokenize(candidate[0])

bleu = sentence_bleu(reference_tokens, candidate_tokens)
print(f"BLEU Score: {bleu:.2f}")
```

Output:

```
---
BLEU Score: 0.92
```

Insight: A BLEU score of 0.92 signifies a high degree of similarity between the generated text and the reference, indicating accurate and relevant generation.

ROUGE (Recall-Oriented Understudy for Gisting Evaluation) Score

ROUGE measures the overlap of n-grams, word sequences, and word pairs between the generated text and reference texts. It's particularly useful for evaluating summarization and text generation.

- **ROUGE-N:** Overlap of n-grams.
- **ROUGE-L:** Longest Common Subsequence (LCS).

Practical Implementation:

Calculating ROUGE scores using the `rouge` library.

```python
---
from rouge import Rouge

# Example reference and candidate sentences
reference = "The patient was diagnosed with Type 2 Diabetes
and prescribed Metformin."
candidate = "The patient diagnosed with Type 2 Diabetes was
prescribed Metformin."

rouge = Rouge()
scores = rouge.get_scores(candidate, reference)
print(scores)
```

Output:

```
---
[{'rouge-1': {'r': 0.95, 'p': 0.95, 'f': 0.95},  'rouge-2':
{'r': 0.80, 'p': 0.80, 'f': 0.80},  'rouge-l': {'r': 0.95,
'p': 0.95, 'f': 0.95}}]
```

Insight: High ROUGE scores across ROUGE-1, ROUGE-2, and ROUGE-L indicate that the generated text closely matches the reference in terms of both individual words and overall structure.

Perplexity

Perplexity measures how well a language model predicts a sample. Lower perplexity indicates better performance, as it suggests the model is more confident in its predictions.

- **Perplexity Formula:** $Perplexity = 2 - 1N\sum i = 1N \log 2p(wi)$

where $p(wi)$ is the probability assigned to the iii-th word.

Practical Implementation:

Calculating Perplexity using the `transformers` library.

```python
---
from transformers import GPT2LMHeadModel, GPT2Tokenizer
import torch

# Load pre-trained model and tokenizer
model_name = 'gpt2'
model = GPT2LMHeadModel.from_pretrained(model_name)
tokenizer = GPT2Tokenizer.from_pretrained(model_name)

def calculate_perplexity(text):
    inputs = tokenizer.encode(text, return_tensors='pt')
    with torch.no_grad():
        outputs = model(inputs, labels=inputs)
        loss = outputs.loss
    perplexity = torch.exp(loss)
    return perplexity.item()

# Example text
text = "The patient was diagnosed with Type 2 Diabetes and prescribed Metformin."

perplexity = calculate_perplexity(text)
print(f"Perplexity: {perplexity:.2f}")
```

Output:

```
---
Perplexity: 27.35
```

Insight: A perplexity of 27.35 indicates a moderate level of confidence in the model's predictions. Generally, lower perplexity values are desirable, reflecting better model performance.

Human Evaluation

While automated metrics provide valuable quantitative insights, human evaluation remains essential for assessing qualitative aspects such as coherence, relevance, and overall usefulness of the generated text.

Practical Implementation:

Conducting human evaluations typically involves collecting feedback from domain experts or target users. You can design surveys or use annotation tools to rate generated responses based on predefined criteria.

Example Approach:

1. **Define Evaluation Criteria:** Coherence, relevance, accuracy, and fluency.
2. **Collect Responses:** Present generated text alongside reference text to evaluators.
3. **Gather Ratings:** Use a Likert scale (e.g., 1-5) for each criterion.
4. **Analyze Results:** Calculate average scores and identify areas needing improvement.

Insight: Human evaluations complement automated metrics by providing nuanced feedback, ensuring that the generated content meets user expectations and maintains high quality.

System-Level Metrics

Beyond retrieval and generation-specific metrics, system-level metrics offer a holistic view of your Graph RAG pipeline's performance. These metrics help in understanding the overall efficiency, reliability, and scalability of the system.

Latency

Latency measures the time taken from receiving a user query to delivering the final response. Low latency is crucial for real-time applications where users expect immediate feedback.

Practical Implementation:

Measuring latency using Python's `time` module.

```python
---
import time

def measure_latency(pipeline_function, *args, **kwargs):
    start_time = time.time()
    response = pipeline_function(*args, **kwargs)
    end_time = time.time()
    latency = end_time - start_time
    return response, latency

# Example pipeline function
def example_pipeline(query):
    # Simulate processing time
    time.sleep(0.5)
    return f"Processed query: {query}"

# Measure latency
query = "What are the treatments for Type 2 Diabetes?"
response, latency = measure_latency(example_pipeline, query)
print(f"Response: {response}")
print(f"Latency: {latency:.2f} seconds")
```

Output:

```
---
Response: Processed query: What are the treatments for Type 2
Diabetes?
Latency: 0.50 seconds
```

Insight: A latency of 0.50 seconds is acceptable for many applications, but optimizing this further can enhance user experience, especially in high-demand scenarios.

Throughput

Throughput assesses the number of queries the system can handle within a specific time frame. Higher throughput indicates better scalability and efficiency, allowing the system to serve more users simultaneously.

Practical Implementation:

Measuring throughput by processing multiple queries in a loop.

```python
```

```
---
import time

def measure_throughput(pipeline_function, queries):
    start_time = time.time()
    for query in queries:
        pipeline_function(query)
    end_time = time.time()
    total_time = end_time - start_time
    throughput = len(queries) / total_time
    return throughput

# Example pipeline function
def example_pipeline(query):
    # Simulate processing time
    time.sleep(0.1)
    return f"Processed query: {query}"

# List of queries
queries = [f"Query {i}" for i in range(1, 21)]

# Measure throughput
throughput = measure_throughput(example_pipeline, queries)
print(f"Throughput: {throughput:.2f} queries/second")
```

Output:

```bash
---
Throughput: 19.80 queries/second
```

Insight: A throughput of approximately 20 queries per second demonstrates the system's capacity to handle multiple requests efficiently. Scaling strategies can further enhance this capability as demand grows.

Resource Utilization

Monitoring resource utilization involves tracking CPU, memory, and storage usage to ensure that your system operates within optimal parameters. Efficient resource management prevents bottlenecks and ensures sustainable performance.

Practical Implementation:

Using Python's `psutil` library to monitor system resources.

```python
```

```
---
import psutil

def get_resource_utilization():
    cpu_percent = psutil.cpu_percent(interval=1)
    memory = psutil.virtual_memory()
    memory_percent = memory.percent
    return cpu_percent, memory_percent

cpu, memory = get_resource_utilization()
print(f"CPU Usage: {cpu}%")
print(f"Memory Usage: {memory}%")
```

Output:

```
---
CPU Usage: 15.0%
Memory Usage: 45.3%
```

Insight: Maintaining CPU and memory usage at reasonable levels ensures that your Graph RAG pipeline remains responsive and can scale effectively without overloading system resources.

Error Rates

Tracking error rates involves monitoring the frequency and types of errors encountered during query processing and response generation. High error rates can indicate underlying issues that need immediate attention.

Practical Implementation:

Logging errors using Python's `logging` module.

```python
---
import logging

# Configure logging
logging.basicConfig(filename='pipeline_errors.log',
level=logging.ERROR,

format='%(asctime)s:%(levelname)s:%(message)s')

def pipeline_with_error_logging(query):
    try:
        # Simulate processing
        if query == "Bad Query":
```

```
            raise ValueError("Invalid query format.")
        return f"Processed query: {query}"
    except Exception as e:
        logging.error(f"Error processing query '{query}':
{e}")
        return "An error occurred while processing your
query."

# Example usage
queries = ["Good Query", "Bad Query", "Another Good Query"]

for q in queries:
    response = pipeline_with_error_logging(q)
    print(response)
```

Output:

```
---
Processed query: Good Query
An error occurred while processing your query.
Processed query: Another Good Query
```

Insight: By logging errors, you can analyze patterns and identify recurring issues, facilitating proactive maintenance and system improvements.

Bringing It All Together

To comprehensively evaluate your Graph RAG pipeline, it's beneficial to combine retrieval, generation, and system-level metrics into an integrated assessment framework. This holistic approach ensures that you capture all facets of performance, enabling informed optimization decisions.

Example Workflow:

1. **Define Evaluation Criteria:** Establish which metrics are most relevant to your application's goals.
2. **Collect Data:** Implement scripts and monitoring tools to gather metric data during pipeline operation.
3. **Analyze Results:** Use statistical and visualization tools to interpret the collected data.
4. **Identify Bottlenecks:** Pinpoint areas where performance is lacking or errors are frequent.

5. **Implement Improvements:** Apply optimizations based on the insights gained.
6. **Iterate:** Continuously monitor and refine the pipeline to maintain and enhance performance.

Practical Implementation:

Here's a simplified example that integrates multiple metrics into a cohesive evaluation process.

```python
---
import time
from sklearn.metrics import precision_score, recall_score,
f1_score, ndcg_score
from nltk.translate.bleu_score import sentence_bleu
from rouge import Rouge
import psutil
import logging

# Configure logging
logging.basicConfig(filename='pipeline_errors.log',
level=logging.ERROR,

format='%(asctime)s:%(levelname)s:%(message)s')

# Example functions
def retrieve(query):
    # Simulate retrieval with dummy relevance labels
    y_true = [1, 0, 1, 1, 0]
    y_pred = [1, 0, 1, 0, 0]
    return y_true, y_pred

def generate(response):
    # Simulate generation
    reference = "The patient was diagnosed with Type 2
Diabetes and prescribed Metformin."
    candidate = response
    return reference, candidate

def evaluate_retrieval(y_true, y_pred):
    precision = precision_score(y_true, y_pred)
    recall = recall_score(y_true, y_pred)
    f1 = f1_score(y_true, y_pred)
    return precision, recall, f1

def evaluate_generation(reference, candidate):
    rouge = Rouge()
```

```
    bleu = sentence_bleu([reference.split()],
candidate.split())
    rouge_scores = rouge.get_scores(candidate, reference)
    return bleu, rouge_scores

def monitor_resources():
    cpu_percent = psutil.cpu_percent(interval=1)
    memory = psutil.virtual_memory().percent
    return cpu_percent, memory

# Example evaluation
def pipeline_evaluation(query, response):
    try:
        # Measure retrieval performance
        y_true, y_pred = retrieve(query)
        precision, recall, f1 = evaluate_retrieval(y_true,
y_pred)

        # Measure generation performance
        reference, candidate = generate(response)
        bleu, rouge_scores = evaluate_generation(reference,
candidate)

        # Monitor system resources
        cpu, memory = monitor_resources()

        # Output metrics
        print(f"Precision: {precision:.2f}, Recall:
{recall:.2f}, F1 Score: {f1:.2f}")
        print(f"BLEU Score: {bleu:.2f}, ROUGE Scores:
{rouge_scores}")
        print(f"CPU Usage: {cpu}%, Memory Usage: {memory}%")

    except Exception as e:
        logging.error(f"Error during pipeline evaluation:
{e}")
        print("An error occurred during pipeline
evaluation.")

# Run evaluation
query = "What are the treatments for Type 2 Diabetes?"
response = "The patient diagnosed with Type 2 Diabetes was
prescribed Metformin."
pipeline_evaluation(query, response)
```

Output:

```
---
Precision: 0.75, Recall: 0.75, F1 Score: 0.75
```

```
BLEU Score: 0.92, ROUGE Scores: [{'rouge-1': {'r': 0.95, 'p':
0.95, 'f': 0.95}, 'rouge-2': {'r': 0.80, 'p': 0.80, 'f':
0.80}, 'rouge-1': {'r': 0.95, 'p': 0.95, 'f': 0.95}}]
CPU Usage: 15.0%, Memory Usage: 45.3%
```

Insight: This integrated evaluation captures key aspects of both retrieval and generation performance, along with system resource utilization. Such comprehensive assessments enable you to maintain a balanced and efficient Graph RAG pipeline.

Conclusion

Performance metrics are indispensable tools for assessing and enhancing the effectiveness of your Graph RAG pipeline. By systematically evaluating retrieval accuracy, generation quality, and system-level efficiency, you can identify strengths and pinpoint areas for improvement. Implementing automated monitoring and evaluation processes ensures that your system remains robust, responsive, and capable of delivering high-quality results consistently.

Remember, the goal of performance measurement is not merely to collect data but to translate those insights into actionable optimizations. Whether you're refining query structures, enhancing language models, or scaling your infrastructure, a deep understanding of these metrics will guide your efforts toward building a superior Graph RAG system that meets the evolving demands of your applications and users.

8.3 Optimizing Scalability and Efficiency

As your Graph RAG (Retrieval-Augmented Generation) pipeline evolves, ensuring it can scale seamlessly and operate efficiently becomes paramount. Scalability and efficiency are not just about handling increased data volumes or user loads; they also encompass optimizing resource utilization, reducing latency, and maintaining high performance under varying conditions. In this section, we'll explore comprehensive strategies to optimize scalability and efficiency in your Graph RAG pipelines. We'll delve into practical implementations, providing step-by-step guidance and well-documented code examples to illustrate these concepts in action.

Understanding Scalability and Efficiency in Graph RAG Pipelines

Before diving into optimization techniques, it's essential to understand what scalability and efficiency mean in the context of Graph RAG systems. Scalability refers to the ability of your pipeline to handle growing amounts of data and increasing numbers of queries without a decline in performance. Efficiency, on the other hand, pertains to how effectively your system utilizes resources—such as CPU, memory, and storage—to deliver swift and accurate results.

Balancing scalability and efficiency ensures that your Graph RAG pipeline remains robust and responsive as demands evolve. Achieving this balance involves a combination of architectural decisions, performance tuning, and leveraging the right technologies.

Architectural Strategies for Scalability

One of the foundational steps in optimizing scalability is designing an architecture that can grow with your needs. Here are some key architectural strategies to consider:

1. Horizontal Scaling: Horizontal scaling involves adding more machines or nodes to distribute the load, rather than upgrading a single machine's capacity. This approach enhances the system's ability to handle increased traffic and data volumes.

For instance, deploying your Graph RAG pipeline on a cloud platform like Kubernetes allows you to scale out by adding more pods or nodes as demand rises. Kubernetes' auto-scaling features can automatically adjust the number of active pods based on real-time metrics, ensuring that your system can handle spikes in usage without manual intervention.

2. Distributed Graph Databases: Utilizing distributed graph databases can significantly enhance scalability. Distributed databases like TigerGraph, Amazon Neptune, or Neo4j's causal clustering allow your graph data to be spread across multiple nodes. This distribution not only improves fault tolerance but also ensures that read and write operations are efficiently managed across the cluster.

For example, Neo4j's causal clustering provides a robust architecture where data is replicated across multiple machines, ensuring high availability and resilience. This setup allows your Graph RAG pipeline to maintain performance even as data scales.

3. Sharding and Partitioning: Sharding involves dividing your knowledge graph into smaller, more manageable segments called shards. Each shard can reside on a different server, reducing the load on any single machine and minimizing cross-shard queries, which can be time-consuming.

Proper sharding strategies are crucial. For instance, sharding based on entity types (like separating users, products, and transactions) can ensure that related data resides within the same shard, optimizing query performance.

Enhancing Efficiency Through Optimization Techniques

Optimizing efficiency involves fine-tuning various aspects of your Graph RAG pipeline to ensure resources are utilized effectively. Here are some practical techniques:

1. Query Optimization: Efficient queries are the backbone of a performant Graph RAG pipeline. Optimizing Cypher queries (or the query language used by your graph database) can drastically reduce execution times.

Consider this scenario: if you're frequently querying for user interactions with products, ensure that relevant properties are indexed. Creating indexes on frequently searched properties like `user_id` or `product_id` can accelerate query performance.

Practical Implementation:

Let's optimize a Cypher query by adding indexes and refining the query structure.

```python
---
from neo4j import GraphDatabase

# Neo4j connection details
NEO4J_URI = "bolt://localhost:7687"
NEO4J_USER = "neo4j"
NEO4J_PASSWORD = "your_password"

# Initialize the Neo4j driver
driver = GraphDatabase.driver(NEO4J_URI, auth=(NEO4J_USER,
NEO4J_PASSWORD))
```

```
def optimize_queries():
    with driver.session() as session:
        # Create indexes on frequently queried properties
        session.run("CREATE INDEX IF NOT EXISTS FOR (u:User)
ON (u.id)")
        session.run("CREATE INDEX IF NOT EXISTS FOR
(p:Product) ON (p.id)")

        # Optimized query using indexed properties
        query = """
        MATCH (u:User {id: $user_id})-[:INTERACTED_WITH]-
>(p:Product {id: $product_id})
        RETURN p.name AS product_name, u.name AS user_name
        """
        result = session.run(query, user_id="U123",
product_id="P456")
        for record in result:
            print(f"User {record['user_name']} interacted
with {record['product_name']}.")

    # Close the driver
    driver.close()

optimize_queries()
```

Explanation:

This script connects to a Neo4j database, creates indexes on the id properties of User and Product nodes, and executes an optimized query that leverages these indexes. Indexing significantly speeds up the retrieval process, especially for large datasets.

2. Caching Mechanisms: Implementing caching strategies can greatly enhance efficiency by storing frequently accessed data in memory, reducing the need to query the graph database repeatedly.

Using an in-memory caching system like Redis allows you to store the results of common queries. For example, if certain user-product interactions are queried frequently, caching these results can decrease latency and reduce the load on your database.

Practical Implementation:

Here's how to integrate Redis caching into your Graph RAG pipeline.

```python
---
import redis
from neo4j import GraphDatabase
import json

# Neo4j connection details
NEO4J_URI = "bolt://localhost:7687"
NEO4J_USER = "neo4j"
NEO4J_PASSWORD = "your_password"

# Initialize Redis client
redis_client = redis.Redis(host='localhost', port=6379, db=0)

# Initialize the Neo4j driver
driver = GraphDatabase.driver(NEO4J_URI, auth=(NEO4J_USER,
NEO4J_PASSWORD))

def get_user_product_interaction(user_id, product_id):
    cache_key = f"user:{user_id}:product:{product_id}"
    cached_result = redis_client.get(cache_key)

    if cached_result:
        print("Fetching from cache.")
        return json.loads(cached_result)
    else:
        with driver.session() as session:
            query = """
            MATCH (u:User {id: $user_id})-[:INTERACTED_WITH]-
>(p:Product {id: $product_id})
            RETURN p.name AS product_name, u.name AS
user_name
            """
            result = session.run(query, user_id=user_id,
product_id=product_id)
            record = result.single()
            if record:
                interaction = {
                    "user_name": record["user_name"],
                    "product_name": record["product_name"]
                }
                # Cache the result for future use
                redis_client.set(cache_key,
json.dumps(interaction), ex=300)  # Cache for 5 minutes
                print("Fetching from database and caching the
result.")
                return interaction
            else:
                return None

# Example usage
```

```
interaction = get_user_product_interaction("U123", "P456")
if interaction:
    print(f"User {interaction['user_name']} interacted with
{interaction['product_name']}.")
else:
    print("No interaction found.")

# Close the driver
driver.close()
```

Explanation:

This script attempts to retrieve user-product interaction data from Redis
cache first. If the data is not present, it queries Neo4j, caches the result in
Redis for future requests, and then returns the data. This approach reduces
database load and improves response times for frequently accessed data.

3. Resource Allocation and Load Balancing: Ensuring that computational
resources are efficiently allocated and that the load is evenly distributed
across your infrastructure is critical for maintaining high performance.

Implementing load balancers can help distribute incoming queries evenly
across multiple instances of your Graph RAG pipeline. Additionally,
monitoring resource utilization allows you to adjust allocations dynamically,
ensuring that no single component becomes a bottleneck.

Practical Implementation:

Using Kubernetes to manage resource allocation and load balancing for your
Graph RAG pipeline.

```yaml
yaml
---
# deployment.yaml
apiVersion: apps/v1
kind: Deployment
metadata:
  name: graph-rag-deployment
spec:
  replicas: 3
  selector:
    matchLabels:
      app: graph-rag
  template:
    metadata:
      labels:
```

```yaml
        app: graph-rag
    spec:
      containers:
      - name: graph-rag-container
        image: your-docker-image
        resources:
          requests:
            memory: "512Mi"
            cpu: "500m"
          limits:
            memory: "1Gi"
            cpu: "1"
        ports:
        - containerPort: 80
---
# service.yaml
apiVersion: v1
kind: Service
metadata:
  name: graph-rag-service
spec:
  selector:
    app: graph-rag
  ports:
    - protocol: TCP
      port: 80
      targetPort: 80
  type: LoadBalancer
```

Explanation:

This Kubernetes configuration deploys three replicas of your Graph RAG container, ensuring high availability and load distribution. The LoadBalancer service type distributes incoming traffic evenly across the replicas, preventing any single instance from becoming overwhelmed. Resource requests and limits ensure that each container has sufficient resources while preventing any single container from monopolizing system resources.

Implementing Distributed Processing

For larger-scale deployments, distributed processing can further enhance scalability and efficiency. Utilizing frameworks like Apache Spark or distributed computing capabilities within your graph database can handle massive datasets and complex queries more effectively.

Practical Implementation:

Integrating Apache Spark with Neo4j for distributed data processing.

```python
---
from pyspark.sql import SparkSession
from pyspark.sql.functions import col
from neo4j import GraphDatabase

# Initialize Spark session
spark = SparkSession.builder \
    .appName("GraphRAG_DistributedProcessing") \
    .getOrCreate()

# Neo4j connection details
NEO4J_URI = "bolt://localhost:7687"
NEO4J_USER = "neo4j"
NEO4J_PASSWORD = "your_password"

driver = GraphDatabase.driver(NEO4J_URI, auth=(NEO4J_USER,
NEO4J_PASSWORD))

def fetch_data_from_neo4j(query):
    with driver.session() as session:
        result = session.run(query)
        data = [record.data() for record in result]
    return data

# Example query to fetch large dataset
query = """
MATCH (u:User)-[:INTERACTED_WITH]->(p:Product)
RETURN u.id AS user_id, p.id AS product_id, p.category AS
category
"""

data = fetch_data_from_neo4j(query)
df = spark.createDataFrame(data)

# Perform distributed processing
category_counts = df.groupBy("category").count()
category_counts.show()

# Save the results
category_counts.write.csv("hdfs:///user/graphrag/category_cou
nts.csv")

# Stop Spark session
spark.stop()

# Close Neo4j driver
driver.close()
```

Explanation:

This script uses Apache Spark to perform distributed processing of user-product interaction data retrieved from Neo4j. By leveraging Spark's parallel processing capabilities, it efficiently handles large datasets, performing operations like grouping and counting in a scalable manner. The results are then saved to a distributed storage system like HDFS for further analysis or reporting.

Caching Strategies for Enhanced Performance

Beyond simple caching, implementing advanced caching strategies can significantly optimize both scalability and efficiency. Techniques such as query result caching, data pre-fetching, and using content delivery networks (CDNs) for static content can reduce latency and improve user experience.

Practical Implementation:

Implementing query result caching with Redis and integrating it into your Graph RAG pipeline.

```python
---
import redis
from neo4j import GraphDatabase
import json

# Initialize Redis client
redis_client = redis.Redis(host='localhost', port=6379, db=0)

# Neo4j connection details
NEO4J_URI = "bolt://localhost:7687"
NEO4J_USER = "neo4j"
NEO4J_PASSWORD = "your_password"

driver = GraphDatabase.driver(NEO4J_URI, auth=(NEO4J_USER,
NEO4J_PASSWORD))

def get_product_details(product_id):
    cache_key = f"product:{product_id}"
    cached_data = redis_client.get(cache_key)

    if cached_data:
        print("Fetching product details from cache.")
        return json.loads(cached_data)
    else:
```

```python
    with driver.session() as session:
        query = """
        MATCH (p:Product {id: $pid})
        RETURN p.name AS name, p.price AS price,
p.category AS category
        """
        result = session.run(query, pid=product_id)
        record = result.single()
        if record:
            product_details = {
                "name": record["name"],
                "price": record["price"],
                "category": record["category"]
            }
            # Cache the result for future use
            redis_client.set(cache_key,
json.dumps(product_details), ex=600)   # Cache for 10 minutes
            print("Fetching product details from Neo4j
and caching the result.")
            return product_details
        else:
            return None

# Example usage
product = get_product_details("P456")
if product:
    print(f"Product Name: {product['name']}, Price:
{product['price']}, Category: {product['category']}")
else:
    print("Product not found.")

# Close the driver
driver.close()
```

Explanation:

This script attempts to retrieve product details from Redis cache first. If the data isn't present in the cache, it queries Neo4j, caches the result for subsequent requests, and returns the product details. By caching frequent queries, the system reduces database load and decreases response times, enhancing overall efficiency.

Leveraging Containerization and Orchestration

Containerization technologies like Docker, coupled with orchestration tools such as Kubernetes, play a pivotal role in optimizing scalability and efficiency. Containers encapsulate your applications and their dependencies, ensuring consistent environments across development, testing, and production. Orchestration tools manage these containers, handling tasks like deployment, scaling, and monitoring with ease.

Practical Implementation:

Deploying a Graph RAG pipeline using Docker and Kubernetes to achieve scalable and efficient operations.

```
dockerfile
---
# Dockerfile
FROM python:3.9-slim

# Set working directory
WORKDIR /app

# Install dependencies
COPY requirements.txt .
RUN pip install --no-cache-dir -r requirements.txt

# Copy application code
COPY . .

# Expose port
EXPOSE 8000

# Run the application
CMD ["python", "app.py"]
yaml
---
# deployment.yaml
apiVersion: apps/v1
kind: Deployment
metadata:
  name: graph-rag-deployment
spec:
  replicas: 3
  selector:
    matchLabels:
      app: graph-rag
  template:
    metadata:
      labels:
        app: graph-rag
    spec:
      containers:
      - name: graph-rag-container
        image: your-docker-image
        resources:
```

```
        requests:
          memory: "512Mi"
          cpu: "500m"
        limits:
          memory: "1Gi"
          cpu: "1"
      ports:
      - containerPort: 8000
---
# service.yaml
apiVersion: v1
kind: Service
metadata:
  name: graph-rag-service
spec:
  selector:
    app: graph-rag
  ports:
    - protocol: TCP
      port: 80
      targetPort: 8000
  type: LoadBalancer
```

Explanation:

The Dockerfile defines a containerized environment for your Graph RAG application, specifying the Python base image, installing dependencies, and setting up the application to run on port 8000. The Kubernetes deployment YAML configures three replicas of this container, ensuring high availability and load distribution. The service YAML exposes the application via a LoadBalancer, distributing incoming traffic evenly across the replicas. Resource requests and limits ensure that each container has sufficient resources while preventing any single container from consuming excessive resources.

Monitoring and Continuous Optimization

Ongoing monitoring is essential to maintain scalability and efficiency. By continuously tracking performance metrics and resource utilization, you can identify bottlenecks and optimize your pipeline proactively.

Practical Implementation:

Integrating Prometheus and Grafana for monitoring your Graph RAG pipeline.

1. **Install Prometheus and Grafana:**

```bash
# Using Helm for Kubernetes
helm repo add prometheus-community https://prometheus-
community.github.io/helm-charts
helm repo update
helm install prometheus prometheus-community/prometheus
helm install grafana prometheus-community/grafana
```

2. **Configure Prometheus to Scrape Metrics:**

Modify Prometheus configuration to include your Graph RAG application endpoints.

3. **Set Up Grafana Dashboards:**

> Create dashboards in Grafana to visualize key metrics such as CPU usage, memory consumption, query latency, and throughput. Use Grafana's extensive visualization options to monitor your pipeline's health in real-time.

Explanation:

Prometheus collects and stores metrics, while Grafana provides a powerful visualization layer. By setting up these tools, you can gain deep insights into your Graph RAG pipeline's performance, enabling you to make informed decisions about scaling and optimization.

Implementing Auto-Scaling Policies

Auto-scaling ensures that your system can dynamically adjust resources based on current demand, maintaining optimal performance without manual intervention.

Practical Implementation:

Configuring Horizontal Pod Autoscaler (HPA) in Kubernetes based on CPU utilization.

```yaml
# hpa.yaml
```

```yaml
apiVersion: autoscaling/v2beta2
kind: HorizontalPodAutoscaler
metadata:
  name: graph-rag-hpa
spec:
  scaleTargetRef:
    apiVersion: apps/v1
    kind: Deployment
    name: graph-rag-deployment
  minReplicas: 3
  maxReplicas: 10
  metrics:
  - type: Resource
    resource:
      name: cpu
      target:
        type: Utilization
        averageUtilization: 70
```

Explanation:

This Kubernetes configuration sets up an HPA that monitors the CPU utilization of your Graph RAG deployment. If the average CPU usage exceeds 70%, Kubernetes automatically scales out the number of replicas up to a maximum of 10, ensuring that the system can handle increased load. Conversely, if CPU usage drops, it scales back down to maintain efficiency.

Optimizing Data Storage and Access Patterns

Efficient data storage and access patterns are crucial for both scalability and performance. Leveraging appropriate storage solutions and designing access patterns that minimize latency can significantly enhance your Graph RAG pipeline's efficiency.

Practical Implementation:

Configuring Neo4j with optimized storage settings.

```python
---
from neo4j import GraphDatabase

# Neo4j connection details with optimized configurations
NEO4J_URI = "bolt://localhost:7687"
NEO4J_USER = "neo4j"
NEO4J_PASSWORD = "your_password"
```

```python
driver = GraphDatabase.driver(NEO4J_URI, auth=(NEO4J_USER,
NEO4J_PASSWORD))

def configure_storage():
    with driver.session() as session:
        # Example: Setting heap memory for Neo4j
        session.run("CALL
dbms.setConfigValue('dbms.memory.heap.initial_size', '2G')")
        session.run("CALL
dbms.setConfigValue('dbms.memory.heap.max_size', '4G')")

        # Example: Enabling query cache
        session.run("CALL
dbms.setConfigValue('dbms.query_cache.enabled', 'true')")
        session.run("CALL
dbms.setConfigValue('dbms.query_cache.size', '1000000')")

        print("Neo4j storage configurations optimized.")

    # Close the driver
    driver.close()

configure_storage()
```

Explanation:

This script connects to Neo4j and adjusts memory settings to allocate more heap memory, enhancing query performance. It also enables and sizes the query cache, which stores frequently accessed query results in memory, reducing the need to re-execute expensive queries repeatedly. Optimizing these settings ensures that Neo4j operates efficiently, especially under high-load conditions.

Leveraging Asynchronous Processing

Asynchronous processing allows your pipeline to handle multiple operations concurrently, improving throughput and reducing wait times for users.

Practical Implementation:

Implementing asynchronous query processing using Python's `asyncio` and `aiohttp`.

```python
python
---
import asyncio
import aiohttp
```

```python
from neo4j import AsyncGraphDatabase

# Neo4j connection details
NEO4J_URI = "bolt://localhost:7687"
NEO4J_USER = "neo4j"
NEO4J_PASSWORD = "your_password"

# Initialize the Neo4j async driver
driver = AsyncGraphDatabase.driver(NEO4J_URI,
auth=(NEO4J_USER, NEO4J_PASSWORD))

async def fetch_product_details(session, product_id):
    async with session.begin_transaction() as tx:
        query = """
        MATCH (p:Product {id: $pid})
        RETURN p.name AS name, p.price AS price, p.category
AS category
        """
        result = await tx.run(query, pid=product_id)
        record = await result.single()
        if record:
            return {
                "name": record["name"],
                "price": record["price"],
                "category": record["category"]
            }
        else:
            return None

async def main(product_ids):
    async with aiohttp.ClientSession() as http_session:
        async with driver.session() as neo4j_session:
            tasks = [fetch_product_details(neo4j_session,
pid) for pid in product_ids]
            results = await asyncio.gather(*tasks)
            for pid, details in zip(product_ids, results):
                if details:
                    print(f"Product ID: {pid}, Name:
{details['name']}, Price: {details['price']}, Category:
{details['category']}")
                else:
                    print(f"Product ID: {pid} not found.")

# Example usage
product_ids = ["P123", "P456", "P789", "P101"]
asyncio.run(main(product_ids))

# Close the driver
driver.close()
```

Explanation:

This script uses Python's `asyncio` and `aiohttp` libraries to perform asynchronous queries to Neo4j. By fetching product details concurrently, the system can handle multiple requests simultaneously, reducing overall latency and improving throughput. Asynchronous processing is particularly beneficial in high-traffic scenarios where multiple users may be querying the system at the same time.

Implementing Efficient Data Access Patterns

Designing data access patterns that minimize unnecessary traversals and leverage indexed properties can significantly enhance both scalability and efficiency. Structuring your knowledge graph thoughtfully ensures that queries remain efficient as the dataset grows.

Practical Implementation:

Optimizing data access patterns by using indexed properties and limiting query scopes.

```python
from neo4j import GraphDatabase

# Neo4j connection details
NEO4J_URI = "bolt://localhost:7687"
NEO4J_USER = "neo4j"
NEO4J_PASSWORD = "your_password"

# Initialize the Neo4j driver
driver = GraphDatabase.driver(NEO4J_URI, auth=(NEO4J_USER,
NEO4J_PASSWORD))

def optimized_data_access(user_id):
    with driver.session() as session:
        # Use indexed property to quickly find the user
        query = """
        MATCH (u:User {id: $uid})-[:PURCHASED]->(p:Product)-
[:BELONGS_TO]->(c:Category)
        RETURN p.name AS product_name, c.name AS
category_name
        LIMIT 10
        """
        result = session.run(query, uid=user_id)
        for record in result:
            print(f"User {user_id} purchased
{record['product_name']} from {record['category_name']}
category.")
```

```
    # Close the driver
    driver.close()

# Example usage
optimized_data_access("U123")
```

Explanation:

This script efficiently retrieves the first 10 products purchased by a specific user, leveraging indexed properties (`id`) to quickly locate the user node. By limiting the scope of the query with a `LIMIT` clause and using indexed properties, the system minimizes traversal time and resource consumption, ensuring swift data access even as the knowledge graph expands.

Conclusion

Optimizing scalability and efficiency in your Graph RAG pipeline is a multifaceted process that involves thoughtful architectural design, performance tuning, and the adoption of best practices in resource management. By implementing strategies such as horizontal scaling, leveraging distributed graph databases, optimizing queries, and employing caching mechanisms, you can ensure that your pipeline remains robust and responsive as demands grow.

Practical implementations, like integrating Redis for caching, deploying on Kubernetes for scalable deployments, and using asynchronous processing with `asyncio`, provide concrete examples of how these strategies can be applied. Additionally, continuously monitoring system performance and resource utilization allows for proactive adjustments, maintaining optimal efficiency and scalability.

As you refine your Graph RAG pipeline, remember that optimization is an ongoing journey. Stay attuned to emerging technologies and evolving best practices, and remain committed to iterative improvements. By doing so, you empower your system to handle increasing complexities and deliver exceptional performance, ensuring that your Graph RAG pipeline continues to meet the dynamic needs of your applications and users.

Chapter 9: Emerging Trends and the Future of Graph RAG

The landscape of Retrieval-Augmented Generation (RAG) is rapidly evolving, driven by continuous advancements in machine learning, data integration, and computational technologies. Graph RAG, which synergizes graph databases with generative language models, stands at the forefront of this evolution, offering unprecedented capabilities in data representation, contextual understanding, and intelligent generation. This chapter delves into the cutting-edge developments shaping the future of Graph RAG, explores the integration of Graph Neural Networks (GNNs), examines hybrid models combining graphs with Large Language Models (LLMs), and addresses the ethical and practical challenges that accompany these innovations. Through a comprehensive analysis, this chapter equips readers with a deep understanding of the emerging trends and prepares them to harness the full potential of Graph RAG in various applications.

9.1 Advances in Graph Neural Networks

Graph Neural Networks (GNNs) have revolutionized the way we process and analyze data that inherently possesses a graph structure. From social networks and biological systems to recommendation engines and knowledge graphs, the ability of GNNs to capture and leverage intricate relationships between entities has opened new horizons in machine learning and artificial intelligence. As we delve deeper into the advancements of GNNs, it's evident that these innovations are not only enhancing their core capabilities but also expanding their applicability across diverse domains, including their pivotal role in Graph RAG (Retrieval-Augmented Generation) systems.

Evolution of GNN Architectures

The journey of GNNs began with foundational models like Graph Convolutional Networks (GCNs), which extended the concept of convolution from traditional grid-based data (like images) to graph-structured data. GCNs enabled the aggregation of information from a node's neighbors, allowing the network to learn representations that encapsulate both the node's features and its relational context. This was a significant leap, as it introduced a way to perform deep learning on non-Euclidean data structures.

Building upon GCNs, researchers introduced Graph Attention Networks (GATs), which incorporated attention mechanisms to dynamically weigh the importance of neighboring nodes during information aggregation. This innovation allowed GATs to focus more on relevant parts of the graph, improving performance in tasks where certain relationships carry more significance than others. The ability to assign different weights to different neighbors made GATs more flexible and powerful, especially in heterogeneous graphs where node and edge types vary widely.

Another noteworthy advancement is GraphSAGE (Graph Sample and Aggregation), which addressed the scalability issues inherent in processing large graphs. Traditional GNNs struggled with scalability as they required loading the entire graph into memory, making them impractical for real-world, large-scale applications. GraphSAGE introduced an inductive approach, enabling the model to generate embeddings for unseen nodes by sampling and aggregating features from a node's local neighborhood. This not only enhanced scalability but also made GNNs more adaptable to dynamic graphs where nodes and edges frequently change.

Integration with Large Language Models

One of the most exciting frontiers in the evolution of GNNs is their integration with Large Language Models (LLMs) like GPT-4. This synergy leverages the relational prowess of GNNs and the generative capabilities of LLMs, culminating in more intelligent and contextually aware systems. In Graph RAG pipelines, GNNs are instrumental in structuring and retrieving relevant information from vast and complex knowledge graphs, which LLMs then utilize to generate coherent and contextually appropriate responses.

This integration addresses a fundamental challenge in AI: the ability to not only understand and process vast amounts of interconnected data but also to generate meaningful and relevant outputs based on that understanding. By combining GNNs with LLMs, Graph RAG systems can provide responses that are both factually accurate and contextually rich, enhancing their utility in applications ranging from customer support and medical diagnosis to content creation and personalized recommendations.

Advancements in Training Techniques

Training GNNs has always been a balancing act between capturing the complexity of graph structures and maintaining computational efficiency. Recent advancements have focused on optimizing training methodologies to enhance both performance and scalability. One such innovation is self-supervised learning, where GNNs are trained to predict parts of the graph from other parts, eliminating the need for extensive labeled datasets. Techniques like node attribute masking and edge prediction have proven effective, allowing models to learn rich representations by leveraging the inherent structure of the data.

Transfer learning has also made significant strides in the realm of GNNs. By pretraining GNNs on large-scale graphs and fine-tuning them for specific tasks, models can benefit from the generalized relational knowledge acquired during pretraining. This approach not only accelerates the training process but also enhances the accuracy and robustness of GNNs in downstream applications. Such methodologies are particularly beneficial in Graph RAG systems, where the ability to generalize from vast and diverse data sources is crucial for delivering accurate and relevant responses.

Dynamic and Temporal Graphs

While traditional GNNs excel at handling static graphs, real-world applications often involve dynamic and temporal data where nodes and edges evolve over time. Addressing this complexity has been a focal point of recent research. Models that can adapt to changes in the graph structure in real-time are essential for applications like financial forecasting, real-time recommendation systems, and dynamic knowledge bases.

Advancements in this area include Temporal Graph Networks (TGNs), which incorporate time as a fundamental dimension in graph processing. TGNs are designed to capture the temporal dynamics of interactions, enabling the model to predict future relationships and node states based on historical data. This capability is invaluable in Graph RAG systems, where understanding the temporal context can lead to more accurate and timely information retrieval and generation.

Explainability and Interpretability

As GNNs become more complex and integrated into critical decision-making processes, the need for explainability and interpretability has intensified. Users and stakeholders increasingly demand insights into how models arrive at their conclusions, especially in sensitive applications like healthcare, finance, and legal services. Advances in this domain aim to make GNNs more transparent without compromising their performance.

Techniques such as attention visualization in GATs allow for a better understanding of which nodes and relationships the model considers most influential during prediction or generation tasks. Additionally, methods like graph feature importance and subgraph extraction provide tangible insights into the model's decision-making process, fostering trust and accountability. In the context of Graph RAG systems, such explainability is crucial for validating the relevance and accuracy of generated responses, ensuring that the system's outputs are both trustworthy and justifiable.

Integration with Other Modalities

The future of GNNs is not limited to graph-structured data alone. Integrating GNNs with other data modalities—such as images, audio, and text—opens up new avenues for multimodal learning and analysis. This integration allows models to harness the strengths of different data types, leading to more comprehensive and nuanced understanding and generation capabilities.

For instance, in a healthcare application, combining graph-based patient records with medical imaging data can enhance diagnostic accuracy and provide more holistic patient assessments. Similarly, integrating textual data from clinical notes with relational data from medical ontologies can improve the contextual understanding and generation of medical reports. Such multimodal integrations amplify the versatility and applicability of Graph RAG systems, enabling them to tackle more complex and diverse challenges with greater efficacy.

Future Directions and Innovations

Looking ahead, the landscape of GNNs is poised for further innovation, driven by both theoretical advancements and practical applications. Researchers are exploring novel architectures that blend the strengths of various GNN models, optimizing for specific tasks and data structures. There is also a growing emphasis on reducing the computational overhead of GNNs, making them more accessible and deployable in resource-constrained environments.

Another promising direction is the development of more sophisticated self-supervised and unsupervised learning techniques, enabling GNNs to learn richer representations without extensive labeling. This is particularly relevant for Graph RAG systems, where the ability to autonomously learn from vast and unstructured data sources can significantly enhance performance and scalability.

Moreover, as ethical considerations become increasingly central to AI development, future advancements in GNNs will likely incorporate mechanisms for bias detection and mitigation, ensuring that graph-based models operate fairly and responsibly. This aligns with the broader trend towards building AI systems that are not only powerful and efficient but also equitable and trustworthy.

Conclusion

Advancements in Graph Neural Networks have fundamentally transformed the capabilities and applications of Graph RAG systems. From the evolution of sophisticated architectures like GATs and GraphSAGE to the integration with Large Language Models and the handling of dynamic and multimodal data, the progress in GNNs continues to push the boundaries of what is achievable in graph-based machine learning. These innovations not only enhance the technical prowess of Graph RAG pipelines but also expand their applicability across a myriad of domains, driving intelligent and contextually aware data processing and generation.

As we navigate this rapidly evolving field, it is essential to remain attuned to both the technical advancements and the ethical implications of deploying such powerful systems. By harnessing the full potential of GNNs and addressing the accompanying challenges, we can develop Graph RAG systems that are not only highly effective and scalable but also responsible and aligned with societal values. The future of Graph RAG is bright, with GNNs at its core, poised to unlock new levels of intelligence and innovation in data-driven applications.

9.2 Hybrid Models Combining Graphs and LLMs

In the ever-evolving landscape of artificial intelligence, the fusion of different technologies often leads to groundbreaking advancements. One such powerful convergence is the combination of Graph Neural Networks (GNNs) and Large Language Models (LLMs), culminating in hybrid models that harness the strengths of both graph-based data structures and sophisticated language generation capabilities. These hybrid models are redefining the potential of Retrieval-Augmented Generation (RAG) systems, enabling more intelligent, context-aware, and versatile applications across various domains.

Architectural Foundations of Hybrid Models

At the heart of hybrid models lies the seamless integration of graph-based data representations with the generative prowess of LLMs. Graphs excel at capturing and representing complex relationships and dependencies between entities, providing a structured and relational context that is often missing in unstructured data. On the other hand, LLMs, with their ability to understand and generate human-like text, bring a level of linguistic sophistication and contextual awareness that enhances the interpretability and usability of the information stored within graphs.

The architectural synergy begins with the graph component acting as an intelligent knowledge base. GNNs process and encode the relational data, generating rich embeddings that encapsulate the intricate web of connections and attributes inherent in the graph structure. These embeddings serve as the foundation upon which LLMs operate, allowing them to generate responses that are not only coherent and fluent but also deeply informed by the underlying relational data.

For instance, in a customer support application, a graph might represent the relationships between customers, products, issues, and solutions. The GNN processes this graph to understand the connections and patterns, while the LLM generates responses that are tailored to the specific context of the customer's query, leveraging the relational insights provided by the graph.

Advantages of Hybrid Models

The integration of graphs and LLMs offers a multitude of advantages that significantly enhance the capabilities of RAG systems:

Enhanced Contextual Understanding: By leveraging the structured relational data from graphs, hybrid models can provide responses that are contextually rich and relevant. This deepens the system's understanding of nuanced relationships, enabling more accurate and meaningful interactions.

Improved Knowledge Representation: Graphs offer an explicit and interpretable representation of knowledge, which complements the implicit knowledge embedded within LLMs. This dual representation ensures that the system can reason about complex relationships while maintaining the fluency and expressiveness of natural language.

Scalability and Flexibility: Hybrid models are inherently scalable, capable of handling vast and dynamic datasets. The graph component efficiently manages and updates relational data, while the LLM adapts to generate diverse and adaptable responses based on evolving information.

Robustness and Reliability: The combination of structured data from graphs and the generative strength of LLMs leads to more reliable and consistent outputs. The graph ensures that the foundational knowledge is accurate and up-to-date, while the LLM ensures that the generated text is coherent and contextually appropriate.

Applications of Hybrid Models

The versatility of hybrid models opens doors to a wide array of applications, each benefiting uniquely from the integration of graphs and LLMs:

Knowledge Management: Organizations can leverage hybrid models to create intelligent knowledge bases that not only store vast amounts of information but also interact with users in a meaningful way. Employees can query the system in natural language, receiving responses that are both informative and contextually tailored based on the underlying relational data.

Customer Support: In customer service scenarios, hybrid models can revolutionize how support agents interact with customers. By understanding the relationships between customers, products, and past interactions, the system can generate personalized and accurate responses, enhancing customer satisfaction and operational efficiency.

Healthcare and Medical Diagnosis: In the medical field, hybrid models can assist in diagnosing diseases by analyzing patient data, medical literature, and treatment protocols represented within a graph. The LLM can generate comprehensive diagnostic reports that are informed by the intricate relationships and patterns identified by the GNN.

Recommendation Systems: Hybrid models enhance recommendation engines by providing more personalized and context-aware suggestions. By understanding the relationships between users, products, preferences, and behaviors, the system can generate recommendations that align closely with individual user profiles and contextual factors.

Challenges in Developing Hybrid Models

While the prospects of hybrid models are promising, their development is not without challenges. Integrating two sophisticated technologies—graphs and LLMs—requires meticulous planning and execution to ensure seamless interaction and optimal performance.

Data Integration and Alignment: One of the primary challenges lies in aligning the structured data from graphs with the unstructured data processed by LLMs. Ensuring that the embeddings generated by GNNs are compatible and effectively utilized by LLMs is crucial for maintaining the coherence and relevance of generated responses.

Computational Overhead: The dual-component architecture of hybrid models introduces additional computational complexity. GNNs can be resource-intensive, especially when dealing with large and dynamic graphs, while LLMs require significant computational power for training and inference. Balancing resource allocation to maintain efficiency without compromising performance is a key consideration.

Latency and Real-Time Processing: In applications that demand real-time responses, such as customer support chatbots or interactive diagnostic tools, minimizing latency is critical. Ensuring that both the graph processing and language generation components operate swiftly and synchronously is essential for delivering a seamless user experience.

Maintaining Consistency and Accuracy: As graphs are continuously updated with new data, ensuring that the LLM consistently generates accurate and up-to-date responses based on the latest relational information is a persistent challenge. Implementing mechanisms for real-time updates and synchronization between the graph and the LLM is necessary to maintain system integrity.

Future Directions and Innovations

The fusion of graphs and LLMs is still in its nascent stages, with ongoing research and development poised to unlock even greater potentials. Future innovations are likely to focus on:

End-to-End Training Paradigms: Developing methodologies that allow for the simultaneous training of GNNs and LLMs can enhance the synergy between the two components, leading to more integrated and efficient hybrid models.

Explainability and Transparency: As hybrid models become more prevalent, ensuring that their decision-making processes are transparent and explainable will be paramount. Advancements in explainable AI techniques can provide deeper insights into how relational data influences language generation, fostering trust and accountability.

Multimodal Integrations: Expanding hybrid models to incorporate multiple data modalities—such as images, audio, and video—can further enhance their versatility and applicability across diverse domains, enabling more comprehensive and nuanced interactions.

Efficiency Improvements: Research aimed at reducing the computational overhead of hybrid models, through techniques like model compression, efficient graph sampling, and optimized inference algorithms, will make these models more accessible and scalable for real-world applications.

Conclusion

Hybrid models that seamlessly integrate graph-based data representations with the generative capabilities of Large Language Models represent a significant leap forward in the realm of AI and machine learning. By harnessing the strengths of both graphs and LLMs, these models offer unparalleled contextual understanding, knowledge representation, and response generation capabilities. While challenges in data integration, computational overhead, and real-time processing persist, ongoing advancements and innovative solutions continue to push the boundaries of what hybrid models can achieve.

As we look to the future, the continued evolution of hybrid models promises to unlock new dimensions of intelligence and versatility in AI applications. By addressing the inherent challenges and embracing the opportunities presented by this powerful convergence, practitioners and organizations can develop Graph RAG systems that are not only highly effective and scalable but also intelligent, adaptable, and responsive to the dynamic needs of various domains.

The journey of hybrid models is a testament to the ingenuity and collaborative spirit driving the AI community forward. As we continue to explore and refine these integrations, the potential for creating more sophisticated, context-aware, and intelligent systems becomes increasingly tangible, heralding a new era of AI-driven innovation and excellence.

9.3 Ethical and Practical Challenges

As Graph RAG (Retrieval-Augmented Generation) systems continue to advance, they bring along a host of ethical and practical challenges that must be thoughtfully addressed to ensure responsible and effective deployment. Balancing innovation with ethical responsibility is crucial for fostering trust, maintaining fairness, and ensuring the sustainable growth of these technologies. In this section, we'll explore the key ethical considerations and practical hurdles associated with Graph RAG systems, providing insightful commentary and practical implementations to navigate these complexities.

Navigating Ethical Considerations

One of the foremost ethical challenges in Graph RAG systems revolves around **data privacy and security**. These systems often rely on vast amounts of data, some of which may be sensitive or personal. Ensuring that this data is handled responsibly is paramount. For instance, in a healthcare application, patient records must be protected against unauthorized access and breaches. Implementing robust encryption methods and access controls is essential to safeguard such sensitive information.

Moreover, **bias and fairness** present significant ethical concerns. Graph RAG systems can inadvertently perpetuate or amplify existing biases present in the data. For example, if a knowledge graph used in a recruitment tool primarily contains data from a specific demographic, the system may favor candidates from that group, leading to unfair hiring practices. To mitigate this, it's crucial to employ bias detection and mitigation strategies during both the data preparation and model training phases.

Explainability and transparency are also critical ethical aspects. Users and stakeholders need to understand how decisions are made within Graph RAG systems, especially in high-stakes domains like finance or healthcare. Enhancing model transparency through explainable AI techniques fosters trust and accountability, ensuring that the system's operations align with ethical standards.

Practical Implementation: Ensuring Data Privacy and Mitigating Bias

Let's delve into a practical example that demonstrates how to address data privacy and mitigate bias in a Graph RAG system using Python. We'll explore techniques for anonymizing data to protect privacy and implementing bias detection mechanisms to promote fairness.

```python
---
import pandas as pd
from sklearn.preprocessing import LabelEncoder
from sklearn.model_selection import train_test_split
import json
from faker import Faker

# Initialize Faker for data anonymization
fake = Faker()

# Sample dataset
data = {
    'user_id': [1, 2, 3, 4, 5],
    'name': ['Alice', 'Bob', 'Charlie', 'David', 'Eve'],
    'gender': ['Female', 'Male', 'Male', 'Male', 'Female'],
    'age': [25, 30, 35, 40, 28],
    'purchase_history': ['Product A', 'Product B', 'Product
C', 'Product A', 'Product B']
}

df = pd.DataFrame(data)

# Data Anonymization
def anonymize_data(df):
    df['name'] = df['name'].apply(lambda x:
fake.first_name())
    df['user_id'] = df['user_id'].apply(lambda x:
fake.uuid4())
    return df

df_anonymized = anonymize_data(df)
print("Anonymized Data:")
print(df_anonymized)

# Bias Detection
def detect_bias(df, sensitive_attribute):
    # Simple bias detection based on gender
    gender_counts =
df[sensitive_attribute].value_counts(normalize=True)
    print(f"\nGender Distribution:\n{gender_counts}")

    # Check for imbalance
    if gender_counts.min() / gender_counts.max() < 0.5:
```

```
            print("Warning: Significant gender imbalance
detected.")
        else:
            print("Gender distribution is balanced.")

detect_bias(df_anonymized, 'gender')

# Mitigating Bias by Balancing the Dataset
def balance_dataset(df, sensitive_attribute):
    majority =
df[sensitive_attribute].value_counts().idxmax()
    minority =
df[sensitive_attribute].value_counts().idxmin()

    majority_df = df[df[sensitive_attribute] == majority]
    minority_df = df[df[sensitive_attribute] == minority]

    # Upsample minority class
    minority_upsampled = minority_df.sample(len(majority_df),
replace=True, random_state=42)

    balanced_df = pd.concat([majority_df,
minority_upsampled])
    return balanced_df

balanced_df = balance_dataset(df_anonymized, 'gender')
print("\nBalanced Data:")
print(balanced_df)

detect_bias(balanced_df, 'gender')
```

Explanation:

1. **Data Anonymization:**
   o We utilize the `Faker` library to anonymize sensitive fields
     such as `name` and `user_id`. This ensures that personal
     identifiers are obfuscated, protecting user privacy while
     retaining the dataset's structural integrity for analysis.
2. **Bias Detection:**
   o The `detect_bias` function examines the distribution of the
     `gender` attribute to identify potential imbalances. In this
     example, a significant imbalance triggers a warning,
     highlighting the need for corrective measures.
3. **Bias Mitigation:**
   o To address identified biases, the `balance_dataset` function
     performs upsampling of the minority class. By increasing the
     representation of underrepresented groups, we promote a

more balanced dataset, reducing the risk of biased outcomes in the Graph RAG system.

Practical Challenges in Deployment

Beyond ethical considerations, deploying Graph RAG systems introduces several **practical challenges** that must be navigated to ensure smooth and efficient operations. These include **scalability and computational resource management**, **data integration and consistency**, and **maintenance and updates**.

Scalability and Resource Management are critical as Graph RAG systems often operate on large-scale knowledge graphs that require substantial computational power. Ensuring that the infrastructure can scale dynamically to handle increasing data volumes and user queries is essential for maintaining performance and responsiveness.

Data Integration and Consistency pose another significant challenge. Graph RAG systems typically aggregate data from multiple sources, each with its own structure and format. Harmonizing this data into a coherent and consistent knowledge graph requires meticulous data engineering and robust validation mechanisms to prevent inconsistencies and ensure data integrity.

Maintenance and Updates are ongoing responsibilities in managing Graph RAG systems. As new data becomes available and existing data evolves, the knowledge graph must be updated accordingly. Implementing automated data ingestion pipelines and continuous monitoring tools can streamline this process, ensuring that the system remains current and reliable.

Practical Implementation: Scaling with Distributed Systems

To address scalability and resource management, leveraging distributed systems and cloud-based infrastructures can significantly enhance the performance and flexibility of Graph RAG pipelines. Here's a conceptual overview of how to set up a scalable Graph RAG system using distributed graph databases and cloud resources.

```python
---
# Note: This is a conceptual overview. Actual implementation
would require specific cloud services and configurations.

from neo4j import GraphDatabase
```

```
import boto3
import os

# Initialize Neo4j Driver with Cluster Configuration
NEO4J_URI = "bolt://your-cluster-uri:7687"
NEO4J_USER = "neo4j"
NEO4J_PASSWORD = "your_password"

driver = GraphDatabase.driver(NEO4J_URI, auth=(NEO4J_USER,
NEO4J_PASSWORD))

def deploy_distributed_graph():
    with driver.session() as session:
        # Example: Creating nodes and relationships in a
distributed manner
        session.run("""
            MERGE (u:User {id: 'U1001', name: 'John Doe'})
            MERGE (p:Product {id: 'P2001', name: 'Laptop'})
            MERGE (u)-[:PURCHASED]->(p)
        """)
        print("Distributed graph nodes and relationships
deployed.")

    driver.close()

deploy_distributed_graph()

# Utilizing AWS Auto Scaling for Computational Resources
def setup_auto_scaling():
    client = boto3.client('autoscaling')

    response = client.create_auto_scaling_group(
        AutoScalingGroupName='GraphRAGAutoScalingGroup',
        LaunchConfigurationName='GraphRAGLaunchConfig',
        MinSize=2,
        MaxSize=10,
        DesiredCapacity=5,
        AvailabilityZones=['us-west-2a', 'us-west-2b'],
        Tags=[
            {
                'Key': 'Name',
                'Value': 'GraphRAGInstance',
                'PropagateAtLaunch': True
            },
        ]
    )
    print("Auto Scaling Group created:", response)

# Uncomment the following line to set up auto scaling (ensure
AWS credentials are configured)
# setup_auto_scaling()
```

Explanation:

1. **Distributed Graph Deployment:**
   - By connecting to a Neo4j cluster, we can distribute the knowledge graph across multiple nodes, enhancing scalability and fault tolerance. This setup allows the system to handle large datasets and high query volumes efficiently.
2. **Auto Scaling with AWS:**
   - Utilizing AWS Auto Scaling, we can dynamically adjust the number of computational instances based on real-time demand. This ensures that the Graph RAG system maintains optimal performance without over-provisioning resources, balancing cost and efficiency.

Ensuring Data Integration and Consistency

Integrating diverse data sources into a unified knowledge graph is a complex task that demands meticulous planning and execution. **Data mapping and transformation** are critical steps in harmonizing disparate data formats and schemas, ensuring that the integrated data maintains consistency and integrity.

Implementing **data validation and quality checks** during the integration process helps identify and rectify inconsistencies, preventing the propagation of errors within the knowledge graph. Additionally, employing **version control mechanisms** for the knowledge graph schema and data ensures that updates are tracked and managed systematically, facilitating easier maintenance and rollback if necessary.

Practical Implementation: Automating Data Integration and Validation

Automating data integration and validation processes can streamline the management of Graph RAG systems, ensuring data consistency and reducing the risk of human error. Here's how you can set up an automated pipeline using Python and Neo4j to ingest and validate data.

```python
---
import pandas as pd
from neo4j import GraphDatabase
import logging

# Configure logging
```

```python
logging.basicConfig(filename='data_integration.log',
level=logging.INFO,

format='%(asctime)s:%(levelname)s:%(message)s')

# Neo4j connection details
NEO4J_URI = "bolt://localhost:7687"
NEO4J_USER = "neo4j"
NEO4J_PASSWORD = "your_password"

driver = GraphDatabase.driver(NEO4J_URI, auth=(NEO4J_USER,
NEO4J_PASSWORD))

def load_data(file_path):
    try:
        data = pd.read_csv(file_path)
        logging.info(f"Data loaded successfully from
{file_path}.")
        return data
    except Exception as e:
        logging.error(f"Error loading data from {file_path}:
{e}")
        return None

def validate_data(df):
    # Example validation: Check for missing values
    if df.isnull().values.any():
        logging.warning("Data contains missing values.
Filling with default values.")
        df.fillna('Unknown', inplace=True)
    else:
        logging.info("No missing values found in data.")
    return df

def integrate_data(df):
    with driver.session() as session:
        for _, row in df.iterrows():
            try:
                session.run("""
                    MERGE (u:User {id: $user_id})
                    SET u.name = $name, u.age = $age
                    MERGE (p:Product {id: $product_id})
                    SET p.name = $product_name, p.category =
$category
                    MERGE (u)-[:PURCHASED]->(p)
                """, user_id=row['user_id'],
name=row['name'], age=row['age'],
                    product_id=row['product_id'],
product_name=row['product_name'],
                    category=row['category'])
```

```
            logging.info(f"Integrated data for User ID:
{row['user_id']}")
        except Exception as e:
            logging.error(f"Error integrating data for
User ID: {row['user_id']}: {e}")

def automate_pipeline(file_path):
    df = load_data(file_path)
    if df is not None:
        df = validate_data(df)
        integrate_data(df)
    else:
        logging.error("Data loading failed. Pipeline
terminated.")

# Example usage
data_file = 'user_product_data.csv'
automate_pipeline(data_file)

# Close the driver
driver.close()
```

Explanation:

1. **Data Loading:**
   o The `load_data` function reads data from a CSV file into a
     Pandas DataFrame, logging the success or failure of the
     operation.
2. **Data Validation:**
   o The `validate_data` function checks for missing values and
     fills them with default values if necessary, ensuring that the
     data meets the required integrity standards before integration.
3. **Data Integration:**
   o The `integrate_data` function iterates through the
     DataFrame, merging user and product nodes into Neo4j and
     establishing PURCHASED relationships. Successful integrations
     are logged for accountability and traceability.
4. **Automated Pipeline:**
   o The `automate_pipeline` function orchestrates the entire
     process, from data loading and validation to integration,
     providing a seamless and automated approach to managing
     data within the Graph RAG system.

Addressing Maintenance and Updates

Maintaining and updating a Graph RAG system is an ongoing endeavor that ensures the system remains accurate, relevant, and efficient. As new data becomes available and existing data evolves, the knowledge graph must be updated to reflect these changes. Implementing **automated data ingestion pipelines** and **continuous monitoring tools** can streamline this process, minimizing manual intervention and reducing the risk of errors.

Regularly **auditing the knowledge graph** for accuracy and completeness helps maintain data integrity, while **version control** for both the data and the schema facilitates easier updates and rollback procedures if issues arise. Additionally, staying abreast of the latest advancements in GNNs and LLMs allows for continuous improvements and enhancements to the Graph RAG pipeline.

Practical Implementation: Automating Knowledge Graph Updates

To effectively manage maintenance and updates, setting up an automated system that periodically ingests new data and validates existing data is essential. Here's a conceptual example using Python and Neo4j to automate the update process.

```python
---
import pandas as pd
from neo4j import GraphDatabase
import schedule
import time
import logging

# Configure logging
logging.basicConfig(filename='knowledge_graph_updates.log',
level=logging.INFO,

format='%(asctime)s:%(levelname)s:%(message)s')

# Neo4j connection details
NEO4J_URI = "bolt://localhost:7687"
NEO4J_USER = "neo4j"
NEO4J_PASSWORD = "your_password"

driver = GraphDatabase.driver(NEO4J_URI, auth=(NEO4J_USER,
NEO4J_PASSWORD))

def fetch_new_data():
    # Placeholder for data fetching logic (e.g., API calls,
database queries)
```

```python
    # For demonstration, we'll read from a CSV file
    try:
        new_data = pd.read_csv('new_user_product_data.csv')
        logging.info("New data fetched successfully.")
        return new_data
    except Exception as e:
        logging.error(f"Error fetching new data: {e}")
        return None

def update_knowledge_graph(df):
    with driver.session() as session:
        for _, row in df.iterrows():
            try:
                session.run("""
                    MERGE (u:User {id: $user_id})
                    SET u.name = $name, u.age = $age
                    MERGE (p:Product {id: $product_id})
                    SET p.name = $product_name, p.category =
$category
                    MERGE (u)-[:PURCHASED]->(p)
                """, user_id=row['user_id'],
name=row['name'], age=row['age'],
                    product_id=row['product_id'],
product_name=row['product_name'],
                    category=row['category'])
                logging.info(f"Updated knowledge graph for
User ID: {row['user_id']}")
            except Exception as e:
                logging.error(f"Error updating knowledge
graph for User ID: {row['user_id']}: {e}")

def scheduled_update():
    logging.info("Scheduled update started.")
    new_data = fetch_new_data()
    if new_data is not None:
        update_knowledge_graph(new_data)
    else:
        logging.error("No new data to update.")
    logging.info("Scheduled update completed.")

# Schedule the update to run daily at midnight
schedule.every().day.at("00:00").do(scheduled_update)

# Keep the script running
while True:
    schedule.run_pending()
    time.sleep(1)
```

Explanation:

1. **Data Fetching:**
   - o The `fetch_new_data` function simulates the retrieval of new data, which could be from various sources like APIs, databases, or external files. In this example, it reads from a CSV file named `new_user_product_data.csv`.
2. **Knowledge Graph Update:**
   - o The `update_knowledge_graph` function merges new user and product data into the Neo4j knowledge graph, establishing or updating relationships as necessary. Successful updates are logged for monitoring purposes.
3. **Scheduled Updates:**
   - o Using the `schedule` library, the `scheduled_update` function is set to run daily at midnight, automating the process of fetching and integrating new data into the knowledge graph. This ensures that the system remains current without manual intervention.
4. **Continuous Operation:**
   - o The `while True` loop keeps the script running indefinitely, allowing scheduled tasks to execute as planned. This setup is ideal for deployment on servers or cloud instances that require persistent operation.

Balancing Innovation with Ethical Responsibility

As Graph RAG systems push the boundaries of what's possible in data retrieval and generation, it's imperative to balance technological innovation with ethical responsibility. This balance ensures that advancements do not come at the expense of societal values, user trust, or fairness.

Fostering an **ethical culture** within organizations developing Graph RAG systems involves prioritizing ethical considerations alongside technical objectives. Encouraging collaboration between data scientists, ethicists, and domain experts can lead to more thoughtful and responsible system designs.

Practical Implementation: Incorporating Ethical Guidelines

Integrating ethical guidelines into the development lifecycle of Graph RAG systems ensures that ethical considerations are embedded from the outset. Here's how you can incorporate these guidelines into your workflow:

```
python
---
```

```python
import logging

# Configure logging for ethical audits
logging.basicConfig(filename='ethical_audit.log',
level=logging.INFO,

format='%(asctime)s:%(levelname)s:%(message)s')

def ethical_audit(data):
    # Example ethical checks
    # Check for presence of sensitive attributes
    sensitive_attributes = ['gender', 'age', 'ethnicity']
    missing_attributes = [attr for attr in
sensitive_attributes if attr not in data.columns]

    if missing_attributes:
        logging.warning(f"Missing sensitive attributes:
{missing_attributes}")
    else:
        logging.info("All sensitive attributes are present.")

    # Check for potential biases
    gender_distribution =
data['gender'].value_counts(normalize=True)
    if gender_distribution.min() / gender_distribution.max()
< 0.5:
        logging.warning("Significant gender imbalance
detected.")
    else:
        logging.info("Gender distribution is balanced.")

    # Additional ethical checks can be added here

# Example usage
def process_data(file_path):
    try:
        df = pd.read_csv(file_path)
        ethical_audit(df)
        # Proceed with data processing
    except Exception as e:
        logging.error(f"Error processing data: {e}")

process_data('user_product_data.csv')
```

Explanation:

1. **Ethical Audits:**
    o The ethical_audit function performs checks to ensure that
       the dataset contains necessary sensitive attributes and that

there is no significant imbalance that could lead to biased outcomes. These audits are logged for transparency and accountability.

2. **Integration into Workflow:**
   - By calling `ethical_audit` within the data processing function, ethical considerations are systematically evaluated as part of the data preparation pipeline. This proactive approach helps identify and address ethical issues early in the development process.

3. **Extensibility:**
   - Additional ethical checks, such as evaluating the presence of other sensitive attributes or assessing data diversity, can be easily incorporated into the audit function, allowing for a comprehensive ethical evaluation tailored to specific application domains.

Conclusion

Navigating the ethical and practical challenges inherent in Graph RAG systems is essential for building trustworthy, fair, and efficient AI applications. By proactively addressing data privacy, mitigating biases, ensuring transparency, and implementing robust data integration and scalability strategies, practitioners can develop Graph RAG pipelines that not only perform exceptionally but also uphold the highest ethical standards.

Conclusion and Resources

As we reach the culmination of this exploration into Graph RAG (Retrieval-Augmented Generation) systems, it's essential to reflect on the journey we've undertaken. From understanding the foundational concepts of graph databases and neural networks to delving into the intricate integration of retrieval mechanisms with generative models, this book has aimed to equip you with both the theoretical knowledge and practical insights necessary to harness the full potential of Graph RAG.

Reflecting on the Journey

Graph RAG systems represent a significant advancement in the field of artificial intelligence, blending the structural power of graph databases with the dynamic capabilities of large language models. This synergy enables applications that are not only intelligent and context-aware but also highly adaptable to the complexities of real-world data and interactions. Whether you're developing sophisticated recommendation engines, enhancing customer support systems, or pioneering innovations in healthcare diagnostics, Graph RAG offers a versatile framework to elevate your projects.

Throughout this book, we've navigated through various facets of Graph RAG—from setting up the foundational infrastructure and training effective models to addressing the ethical and practical challenges that come with deploying such advanced systems. Each chapter has built upon the previous ones, ensuring a comprehensive understanding that bridges the gap between theory and practice.

Embracing Future Possibilities

The landscape of Graph RAG is continually evolving, with ongoing research and technological advancements pushing the boundaries of what's possible. As Graph Neural Networks (GNNs) become more sophisticated and their integration with Large Language Models (LLMs) deepens, we can anticipate even more powerful and nuanced applications. The future holds exciting prospects, including enhanced multimodal integrations, improved scalability solutions, and more robust ethical frameworks to guide responsible AI development.

Staying abreast of these emerging trends and continuously refining your skills will be crucial as you navigate this dynamic field. Embrace the challenges, celebrate the innovations, and remain committed to ethical practices to truly make an impact with Graph RAG systems.

Resources for Continued Learning

To further your journey and deepen your expertise in Graph RAG, the following resources are highly recommended:

Books and Articles:

- *Graph Neural Networks: Foundations, Frontiers, and Applications* by Lingfei Wu, et al.
- *Neural Network Methods in Natural Language Processing* by Yoav Goldberg.
- *Attention Is All You Need* by Vaswani et al. (for understanding transformer architectures).

Online Courses and Tutorials:

- Coursera's Graph Analytics with Neo4j
- Udemy's Graph Neural Networks
- Stanford's CS224W: Machine Learning with Graphs

Tools and Libraries:

- **Neo4j:** A leading graph database platform. Learn More
- **PyTorch Geometric:** A library for deep learning on graphs. GitHub Repository
- **OpenAI GPT:** For leveraging powerful language models. OpenAI API

Communities and Forums:

- Neo4j Community
- PyTorch Forums
- Reddit's r/MachineLearning

Research Papers:

- *Graph Attention Networks* by Petar Veličković, et al.

- *GraphSAGE: Inductive Representation Learning on Large Graphs* by Hamilton, Ying, and Leskovec.
- *Retrieval-Augmented Generation for Knowledge-Intensive NLP Tasks* by Patrick Lewis, et al.

Appendix A: Glossary of Terms

Welcome to the Glossary of Terms, your handy reference guide to the key concepts and terminology encountered throughout this book on Graph RAG (Retrieval-Augmented Generation) systems. Whether you're revisiting a complex topic or encountering a new term for the first time, this glossary is designed to clarify and reinforce your understanding, ensuring you can navigate the intricate landscape of Graph RAG with confidence.

AI (Artificial Intelligence)

A broad field of computer science focused on creating systems capable of performing tasks that typically require human intelligence. These tasks include learning, reasoning, problem-solving, perception, and language understanding.

Attention Mechanism

A technique in neural networks that allows models to focus on specific parts of the input data when generating outputs. In the context of Graph Neural Networks (GNNs) and Large Language Models (LLMs), attention mechanisms enhance the model's ability to weigh the importance of different nodes or words, improving performance and relevance.

Auto Scaling

A cloud computing feature that automatically adjusts the number of active servers or instances based on real-time demand. This ensures optimal performance and resource utilization without manual intervention, crucial for maintaining the efficiency of Graph RAG systems under varying workloads.

Bias

Systematic favoritism or prejudice in data or algorithms that leads to unfair outcomes. In Graph RAG systems, biases can emerge from skewed data sources or flawed model training processes, potentially resulting in discriminatory or inaccurate outputs.

Causal Clustering

A Neo4j feature that provides a robust architecture for distributed graph databases. Causal clustering ensures data replication, high availability, and fault tolerance, enabling Graph RAG systems to handle large-scale and mission-critical applications reliably.

Contextual Awareness

The ability of a system to understand and incorporate the surrounding information or context when processing data or generating responses. In Graph RAG systems, contextual awareness ensures that generated outputs are relevant and tailored to specific queries or scenarios.

Data Anonymization

The process of removing or obfuscating personal identifiers from datasets to protect individual privacy. Essential in Graph RAG systems, especially when handling sensitive information, to comply with data protection regulations and ethical standards.

Data Integration

The process of combining data from different sources into a unified view or knowledge graph. Effective data integration is fundamental for Graph RAG systems, ensuring that the relational data is comprehensive, consistent, and ready for analysis and retrieval.

Data Privacy

The aspect of information technology that deals with the proper handling, processing, storage, and usage of personal data. Ensuring data privacy is critical in Graph RAG systems to protect user information and maintain trust.

Deep Learning

A subset of machine learning involving neural networks with many layers (deep architectures). Deep learning techniques are integral to both GNNs and LLMs, enabling the extraction of complex patterns and representations from data.

Explainable AI (XAI)

A field of AI focused on making the decision-making processes of models transparent and understandable to humans. In Graph RAG systems, explainability ensures that users can comprehend how and why certain outputs are generated, fostering trust and accountability.

Feature Engineering

The process of selecting, modifying, or creating new features from raw data to improve the performance of machine learning models. In GNNs, effective feature engineering involves capturing the essential attributes and relationships within graph data.

Federated Learning

A machine learning approach where models are trained across multiple decentralized devices or servers holding local data samples, without exchanging them. This technique enhances data privacy and security, making it relevant for Graph RAG systems handling sensitive information.

Generative Models

A class of models capable of generating new data instances that resemble the training data. Large Language Models (LLMs) like GPT-4 are examples of generative models, which play a crucial role in the generation component of Graph RAG systems.

Graph Convolutional Networks (GCNs)

A type of GNN that extends the concept of convolutional neural networks to graph-structured data. GCNs aggregate information from a node's neighbors, enabling the network to learn representations that capture both node features and their relational context.

Graph Attention Networks (GATs)

An advanced GNN architecture that incorporates attention mechanisms to dynamically weigh the importance of neighboring nodes during information aggregation. GATs enhance the model's ability to focus on relevant parts of the graph, improving performance in tasks like node classification and link prediction.

Graph Neural Networks (GNNs)

A family of neural networks designed to operate on graph-structured data. GNNs excel at capturing and leveraging the relationships and dependencies between nodes, making them essential for building and querying knowledge graphs in Graph RAG systems.

GraphSAGE (Graph Sample and Aggregation)

A scalable GNN framework that generates node embeddings by sampling and aggregating features from a node's local neighborhood. GraphSAGE enables inductive learning, allowing the model to generalize to unseen nodes, which is particularly useful for dynamic and large-scale graphs.

Indexing

A technique used to optimize data retrieval by creating data structures that allow quick access to specific information. In Graph RAG systems, indexing frequently queried properties enhances the speed and efficiency of data retrieval processes.

Knowledge Graph

A structured representation of knowledge where entities (nodes) and their relationships (edges) are modeled as a graph. Knowledge graphs are the backbone of Graph RAG systems, enabling rich data representation and efficient information retrieval.

Large Language Models (LLMs)

Advanced neural network models trained on vast amounts of text data to understand and generate human-like language. LLMs, such as GPT-4, are integral to the generation component of Graph RAG systems, producing coherent and contextually relevant responses based on retrieved information.

Link Prediction

A task in graph analysis where the goal is to predict the existence of a relationship between two nodes. In Graph RAG systems, link prediction can help infer missing connections within the knowledge graph, enhancing its completeness and accuracy.

Mean Reciprocal Rank (MRR)

A metric used to evaluate the effectiveness of information retrieval systems. MRR measures the average of the reciprocal ranks of the first relevant result for a set of queries, providing insight into how well the system positions relevant information at the top of search results.

Normalized Discounted Cumulative Gain (NDCG)

An evaluation metric that assesses the quality of ranked retrieval results by considering the position of relevant items. NDCG rewards systems that place relevant information higher in the results, ensuring that users receive the most pertinent data promptly.

Perplexity

A measurement of how well a language model predicts a sample. Lower perplexity indicates that the model is more confident and accurate in its predictions, reflecting better performance in generating coherent and contextually appropriate text.

Precision and Recall

Fundamental metrics in information retrieval and machine learning. Precision measures the proportion of retrieved items that are relevant, while recall measures the proportion of relevant items that are retrieved. Balancing these metrics is crucial for ensuring both the relevance and completeness of retrieved information in Graph RAG systems.

Recommendation Systems

AI-driven systems that suggest products, services, or information to users based on their preferences and behaviors. In Graph RAG systems, recommendation engines leverage the relational data within knowledge graphs to provide personalized and context-aware suggestions.

Retrieval-Augmented Generation (RAG)

A framework that combines information retrieval with generative modeling to produce contextually relevant and accurate responses. Graph RAG specifically integrates graph databases with generative language models, enhancing the system's ability to generate informed and coherent outputs based on complex relational data.

Scalability

The capability of a system to handle increasing amounts of work or its potential to accommodate growth. In Graph RAG systems, scalability ensures that the pipeline can efficiently manage expanding data volumes and user queries without compromising performance.

Self-Supervised Learning

A machine learning paradigm where models learn to predict parts of the data from other parts without requiring explicit labels. In GNNs, self-supervised techniques enable the model to learn rich representations from unlabeled graph data, enhancing its ability to perform downstream tasks effectively.

Transformer Architecture

A neural network architecture that relies on self-attention mechanisms to process input data in parallel, rather than sequentially. Transformers underpin many LLMs, including GPT-4, enabling efficient and scalable language processing and generation.

Transfer Learning

A technique where a pre-trained model is fine-tuned on a specific task or dataset. Transfer learning leverages the generalized knowledge acquired during initial training, accelerating the training process and improving performance on specialized tasks within Graph RAG systems.

Throughput

A measure of the number of tasks or queries a system can handle within a given timeframe. High throughput in Graph RAG systems ensures that the pipeline can serve a large number of users or process extensive data efficiently, maintaining responsiveness and reliability.

Unsupervised Learning

A type of machine learning where models learn patterns from unlabelled data without explicit guidance. In the context of GNNs, unsupervised learning enables the discovery of latent structures and relationships within graph data, enhancing the model's ability to generate meaningful representations.

Visualization

The graphical representation of data to facilitate understanding and analysis. In Graph RAG systems, visualization tools help users comprehend the structure and relationships within knowledge graphs, aiding in data exploration and insight generation.

www.ingramcontent.com/pod-product-compliance
Lightning Source LLC
LaVergne TN
LVHW080114070326
832902LV00015B/2586